Presented to:

‗‗‗‗‗‗‗‗‗ D1714346 ·

By:

_____

Date: _____

"Have you ever had a dream... that you were so sure was real? What if you were unable to wake from that dream? How would you know the difference between the dream world and the real world? ... You're here because you know something. What you know you can't explain, but you feel it. ... You don't know what it is, but it's there, like a splinter in your mind, driving you mad. ... Do you know what I'm talking about? – Morpheus (The Matrix)

"Good fiction is made of what is real, and reality is difficult to come by." – Ralph Ellison

"Fiction is a lie, and good fiction is the truth inside the lie." – Stephen King

"The truth is like a lion; you don't have to defend it. Let it loose; it will defend itself." – Augustine of Hippo

"Those who are able to see beyond the shadows and lies of their culture will never be understood, let alone believed, by the masses." – Plato

"The smarter mysteries are hidden in the light" – Jean Giono

"This is the West, sir. When the legend becomes fact, print the legend." – Newspaperman Maxwell Scott to Ransom Stoddard (The Man Who Shot Liberty Valance)

"There's always room for a story that can transport people to another place" - J.K.Rowling

Is this the real life? Is this just fantasy? – Freddi Mercury

"We consider it a good principle to explain the phenomena by the simplest hypothesis possible." – Ptolemy

Listen, then make up your own mind." – Gay Talese

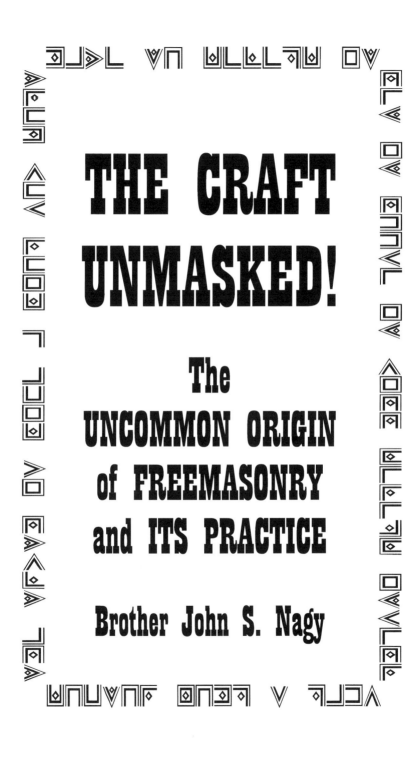

THE CRAFT UNMASKED!

The UNCOMMON ORIGIN of FREEMASONRY and ITS PRACTICE

Brother John S. Nagy

The Craft Unmasked – The Uncommon Origin of
Freemasonry and Its Practice
Copyright © 2014 Dr. John S. Nagy

Also Author of:
Building Hiram – Volume 1
Building Boaz – Volume 2
Building Athens – Volume 3
Building Janus – Volume 4
Building Perpends – Volume 5
Building Ruffish – Volume 6
Building Cement – Volume 7
Building Free Men – Volume 8
Provoking Success
Emotional Awareness **Made Easy**

Publisher: Promethean Genesis Publishing
PO Box 636, Lutz FL 33548-0636

ISBN-13: 978-0-9911094-2-5

Second Printing, Dec. 2014
Published in the United States of America
Book Editing, Design and Illustration
by Dr. John S. Nagy
Books available through www.coach.net

Dedication

To my Brother Builders Jeff, Dale, Jason, Albert, Michael, Nick, R.J., Luther, Jon, Richard and Tom: I offer a sincere and heartfelt *thank you* for helping to reveal this book.

To my future Brother Builders: may this book help Light your way as you continue your Journey East, Masterfully Building.

To my two sons: I look forward to the day you Rise in Mastery so that I may gift this book to you as Masterful Men.

To my loving and supportive wife and best friend: when you say, "Right!" I have to agree.

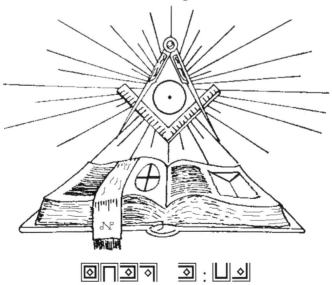

"How is the history of Freemasonry to be written, so that the narrative shall win the respect of its enemies[1], and secure the assent and approbation of its friends? In the first place, we must begin by a strict definition of the word Masonry. If we make it synonymous with Freemasonry, then must we confine ourselves closely to the events that are connected with the Institution in its present form and organization. ...

"... No greater honor could accrue to any man than that of having been the founder of a new school of Masonic history, in which the fictions and loose statements of former writers would be rejected, and in which the rule would be adopted that has been laid down as a vital maxim of all inductive science, — in words that have been chosen as his motto by a recent powerful investigator of historical truth:

'Not to exceed and not to fall short of facts — not to add and not to take away. To state the truth, the whole truth, and nothing but the truth.'" [2]

– *Bro. Albert C. Mackey 33° (History of Freemasonry; Encyclopedia of Freemasonry, 1917 edition)*

SUITABLE & FAIR WARNINGS

1) This document contains a series of critical connections that might at first <u>cause emotions of extreme discomfort, disgust, irritation, shock, and dismay</u>, especially if you are a member of the Society of Free & Accepted Masons. It is highly recommended that you read through the entire book before you draw any rash, superficial and wholly unsupported conclusions. Your efforts shall be rewarded!

2) As with all Freemasonic Ritual, where it is always best not to discuss anything therein contained with anyone who has yet to experience it legitimately, fully and completely, it is highly recommended that you not discuss anything within this book with anyone who has yet to read it thoroughly & completely for himself. Doing  so, <u>revealing anything in this book to others who have yet to read it, shall both ruin the intended experience of the book for them and prevent you from having a rich discussion about it with an informed person</u>.

3) As of the first publishing of this book, no Grand Lodge exists today that publically or privately shares this author's view of the Origin and Practices of the Society of Free & Accepted Masons.

Preface

*The Words before you are those that I wish
I had Received before I was first Dramatically
Introduced to the Workings of the Craft.*

There is no doubt whatsoever that the Craft has been around since Time Immemorial. It has been used by many societies to help transform those individuals within them for the better and in ways that many have yet to begin to imagine. It is so powerful a Craft that even many of the numerous Craft Keepers themselves are truly unaware of the Craft basis that helps contribute to the welfare of humanity through their Principled Practices.

Yet, even though the Craft is hidden in plain sight, the *Mystery of Masonry* escapes the understanding of far too many of its members and non- Craft members. This doesn't prevent individuals from practicing it and benefiting from its practice. Such benefits are a direct result of its application and it doesn't require an awareness or understanding of the Craft, *just a Mastering of it.* The Craft is that Empowering.

Many have come to its Quarry. Many have Mastered its ways. Many have profited from its Practice. But, few actually Understand what they are truly doing. *Somehow, along the way, the Craftsmen have forgotten what their Craft actually is and for what Purpose it is Practiced.*

Definitions [3]

Pre-Mason – Those who are destined to become Societal members who have yet to be Made.

Made – Initiated; Accepted; Archaic word for having Joined, Entered the Society.

Mason – A Builder

Free Mason – A Superior or Excellent Builder

Masonry – The Art and Science of Building

Freemason – a Member of the *Society of Free & Accepted Masons;* an Accepted Mason.

Freemasonry – The Organizational Structures, Rules, Laws, Traditions, Lore, and Rituals that support the Practices of the Freemasonic Society.

Candidates – Paying Patrons who play central parts & main characters in Lodge Performances.

Lodge – members of a part of the Society who Perform Rituals at approved locations and as a unit.

Degrees – Performances that Patrons experience at specific levels of Organizational membership.

Ritual[4] – Promulgated and Canonized Scripts.

Lectures – Infotainment written by a variety of Creative Authors originally used to entice Patrons to join specific Lodges and to continue to return**.**

Officers – supportive Cast of Characters needed for routine Ritual Performances and to manage Lodge assets.

Sideliners – Lodge Members who take on the audience role and who provide auxiliary support at times for Performance success.

Open Book – Where Peculiar Scripts are held and reviewed for periodic reference.

Cipher/Code Book – Scripts written to prevent untrained observers from understanding them.

Peculiar[5] – Privately owned; exclusive to

Morality[6] – 1. principles concerning the distinction between right and wrong or good and bad behavior. 2. Staged plays intended and designed to convey mores.

Pomp – 1. stately or splendid display; splendor; magnificence. 2. ostentatious or vain display, esp. of dignity or importance. 3. pompous displays, actions, or things. 4. [Archaic] a stately procession; pageant.

Tragedy – **1**. an event causing great suffering, destruction, and distress, such as a serious accident, crime, or natural catastrophe. 2. a play dealing with tragic events and having an unhappy ending, especially one concerning the downfall of the main character. 3. the dramatic genre represented by tragedy.

Sublime[7] – 1. of such excellence, grandeur, or beauty as to inspire great admiration or awe. 2. used to denote the extreme or unparalleled nature of a person's attitude or behavior. 3. [Archaic] elevate to a high degree of moral or spiritual purity or excellence.

Fossick[8] – 1. To search for gold or gemstones typically by picking over discarded or abandoned workings and materials. 2. To search about or rummage. 3. To ferret out.

West Gate – The point of Entrance for all Blue Lodge Degree Candidates.

Blue Lodges – also known as Symbolic Lodges. Those Lodges who Perform the First Three Degrees associated with the York Rite.

York Rite – Degree style Performances that continue the Story line introduced to Blue Lodge Candidates.

Scottish Rite – Degree style Performances that continue the Philosophies introduced to Blue Lodge Candidates.

Hypocrisy[9]– the practice of claiming to have moral standards or beliefs to which one's own behavior does not conform; pretense; fraud

The Craft – 1. The Whole of Freemasonic Practice. 2. Those who collectively Practice Freemasonry

The Word:

It Cannot Be
Given to You.

It Cannot Be
Obtained
from Others.

It can only
Be Authentically
Portrayed, for It
To Be Real.

Table of Contents

Introduction

All the Lodge's a Stage,
And all the Brothers merely players;[10]

For many days I sat before my keyboard numb and dumbfounded with the sheer magnitude of that which I was about to write. The words, *"where do I begin"* kept whirling around in my head and they were interrupted only momentarily by random insights. I was overwhelmed by the daunting tasks that lie ahead and knew that I must press on, quickly putting bits and pieces down as I captured them in fleeting moments of clarity. The many interrelated issues that interconnect with Masonic memories continued to appear with every word I typed.

The whole picture portraying Freemasonry was becoming clearer. The words and phrases that were there from the beginning and that I thought meant only one thing turned and twisted in directions that I could only now begin to comprehend. All of this was masterfully hidden in plain sight for all those to see as it existed for nearly three hundred years. The Craft has remained blind to what was clearly a Masterful rendering put forth with the best of intentions.

Background

From the time I first was introduced to Freemasonic Ritual, I knew there was something more to it than just a bunch of interesting concepts thrown together. After I joined the Society and settled into its routine activities, I began to explore. I set out to uncover the personal development maps that each Blue Lodge Degree reveals to Better Good men. I successfully decoded each and rendered the maps in book form, showing many of the roots of many of the symbols, words and phrases. I uncovered historical connections to many of these symbols, words and phrases, making these Rituals all the more precious. I unraveled the many tangled ropes that make up these Rituals, allowing for a straighter course to recognize the significance of many Ritual elements. This enabled members of the Society to understand them more in depth, and to apply them toward Betterment of themselves. I opened up many doors to personal development for Brothers who worked along with me. Some Brothers contributed much to my efforts by challenging my discoveries, asking questions based upon what was discovered. This feedback catalyzed further discoveries. They supported my efforts by investing in the Works I rendered for them.

With these efforts and my Brothers' encouragement, came eight Masonic Education books. They specifically detailed Ritual elements that direct men toward things that they could and should do to improve themselves as good men. I drew a verbal roadmap of what the Blue Lodge Degrees directed men to do to improve themselves Emotionally, Intellectually and Spiritually. It was quite an undertaking and well worth it.

I also found inconsistencies in some of the definitions of words and phrases shared by Brothers and by Grand Lodges that unnecessarily distracted men from concepts and ideas that would further them in their Betterment efforts. I uncovered the origins of words like *Cowan, Freemason, Accepted,* and *Freeborn*[11] that, when understood as they were meant originally, shed an entirely different light upon what is currently occurring within the Society.

In these exploration, discovery, and recovery efforts, I also broke away from my focus upon Ritual and ventured into the history of the Craft. That information triggered a series of other actions that ultimately led to the creation of this book.

I had no idea what this book ultimately would look like when I started writing my notes. The information I gathered presented a view of the Craft that was unique and perhaps Transformative for the Better and in ways that I can now only hesitate to imagine.

I offer to you in advance an apology for putting what I found into print. Should you choose to continue to read it all the way through, your view of Freemasonry shall forever change. Hopefully, that change shall be for the Better and shall assist you in its Practice for years to come.

The Initial Shock

When I first came across the information that would become this book, I confess that I felt betrayed. I thought that I was the brunt of a huge joke perpetrated upon millions of men over hundreds of years. I continually asked myself, "How could this be?" The shock made my head swim.

To be frank, I became depressed. Something that seemed so firm in my heart and mind crumbled before my eyes and I was unprepared for it. To add to my situation, no one was there to help me sort the shattered pieces. No one was there to help me make sense of it. I was alone in what I saw and I felt that isolation.

I didn't stop and stay idle though. Once I came to understand what I had discovered, I began to ask different questions of myself. How could something so basic not be embraced and used to the Craft's benefit? How could something that is Practiced in Blue Lodges all around the globe not be fundamentally taught as part of Craft Training and done so with great zeal and exuberance?

More Light

As I explored and wrote about the topic further, I had a change of heart. I saw the wisdom behind what could be perceived as a very large deception. I came to a very startling realization that what I had participated in could not possibly have been put together in any other way. As it is constructed, it helps preserve and perpetuate a treasure trove of directions that men need to improve themselves.

Simple in its deliverance and Masterful in its design, the Craft does indeed do what it set out to do and in Grand fashion.

Simply Masterful it is in every way and in ways that the majority have not recognized and understood, till now.

Enjoy!

Bro. John S. Nagy

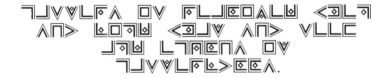

Precursory Notes:

1. The themes and concepts presented within this book are intended to stir discourse between Brothers and provoke thought on the Work Freemasons should do and hopefully Master. It is also intended to encourage Freemasons to Progress as they could and as they should.
2. It is recommended that readers of this book familiarize themselves with the terms found in its pages. Context is everything and enhances their meaning.
3. Although the information contained within these pages *did not come from present day Ritual,* the Light herein offered though is still significant today.
4. The resources that helped create this book are freely available to anyone so interested and for those who earnestly seek them.
5. This writing explains no present day Freemasonic Ritual. No Penetralia are revealed within this book nor does it point to anything that is not already known to all who seek Light. **If you are looking to find secrets, Freemasonic or otherwise, there are none herein for you to find.**
6. Should you desire to use this material in your Lodge, do so in accordance with the Laws of your Jurisdiction.
7. *Knowledge is inventory, not Power, and it's useless unless properly applied.* The 3rd Degree Legend points toward Work that was done. *Knowing is not enough. Work must be done.*
8. Finally, all that is presented herein is found in Symbolic Lodge Masonry and related books.

I. The Grand Assumption

So many Seekers assume that Freemasonry comes from Roots that are somehow Disclosed by or Alluded to within its very Rituals and Lectures. Unfortunately, the very Craft Freemasonry conceals is done so well that it required no hiding at all!

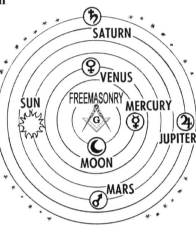

From all that is written about Freemasonry, one could conclude quite safely that the Society from its very beginning has masked its origins with Masterful veils. One could also easily conclude that it was purposefully done this way as to take focus off its primary roots. Such conclusions are easily supported by the overwhelming lack of consistency among the multitudes of theory surrounding the Craft built up by years of conjectures from hundreds of zealous authors.

Along these same lines, anyone removing these carefully placed layers would not find revealed any deceit or deception. They would not find a terrible grand conspiracy of any sort. They would find, as with every Masterful Production, Freemasonry's intention to accomplish something wonderfully grand.

It is profusely clear that the Freemasonic Organization was a truly Masterful way to do something that was life changing for any generation.

There is one constant within these writings which stands out as a beacon leading many members and non members to crash upon the rocky shores of self-deception. That one consistency is the assumption that the Freemasonic Organization came from any origin other than the one that could be most obvious to an unbiased observer.

Far too many have accepted without question the offerings of those who have come before them. Equally, far too many have not stepped back and actually observed what the Craft was actually doing. As a result, when faced with investigating Craft origins, they start out upon their quest on a biased road and in directions that lead them toward further illusions.

From the Society's very beginning, one specific assumption was made by almost every member Entering the Craft. From then on that one assumption has had each member redirect his thoughts away from its true origins and toward historical fantasies that had little to do with Craft origins.

A Brotherly Light House

Brother Albert Mackey had a good sense that this was the case. His thoughts on investigating Craft origins are captured in a few of his attributed writings on Freemasonic history. He was not kind in what he had to say about many of the authors of his time, or those whom preceded it. Brother Mackey states very concisely that to write Freemasonry's history, one must first take extreme care in how one defines it. He goes on to convey that it is also clear that to include Masonry in this writing, it must not be taken to be synonymous with Freemasonry unless *"we confine ourselves closely to the events that are connected with the Institution in its present form and organization"*. Our Brother also tells us that far too many authors use the word

16

"Masonry" loosely. He provides several examples of this looseness and he then summarily dismisses their contributions as a result. His message is a warning that very few have heeded, even to this day.

I believe he conveyed great wisdom. I also believe his observations and conclusions were brilliant on this issue but he did not go far enough in his statements. He did however reveal the path to future Craft origin discovery for those who would follow his works.

Tagging Along

A few years back, I began to see that there was a difference between how some of the words associated with Freemasonry and Masonry were being used. Sometimes they were being used synonymously. Other times they would change their meaning each time they were being used, even within the same sentence. The inconsistency of this was enough to grab my attention and hold it. And I would find that I was not alone in this observation.

Within a very short time, I had gathered enough information to conclude that the two words were entirely different in their focus. I also concluded that there exist many people, in particular Brothers, who take them to mean the same thing. Included in this latter group are many of the writers that help shape the psyche of each generation, inside and outside the Society.

Furthermore, not only did they take these two words to be synonymous, but they used them interchangeably and with shear irreverence to their roots. In that acceptance, they were blind to their blatant differences. With every sentence they wrote, they soon could not see any difference whatsoever as they employed these words in their writings.

I began to share my observations about these two words with others. I first did this with those who expressed to me their confusion as to what the Society was actually doing. We seemed to have come to the same conclusions along similar lines of investigation. It was a breath of relief for all who engaged in these thought exchanges. In a very warm way what we saw was being confirmed through our interactions.

This validation brought about a bit of boldness on all our parts and we began sharing our thoughts and conclusions with others outside our circles when opportunities arose. It was amazing to us how we would get such a mix of responses to our disclosers.

Some listeners simply nodded their heads in understanding. It was clear to us by their response that they saw and believed the same things. You could see in their countenances, and more specifically their eyes, how much they appreciated our putting words to what they intuitively felt. It was an awesome experience for all of us.

Brotherly Ugliness

There was also a dark side to all this. There were some self-appointed protectors of the Craft that took exception to our sharing. They found it annoying and antagonistic to what they had come to believe about the Fraternity. In response, they reacted very negatively to any and all sharing that was contrary to what they themselves had accepted to be true.

Sometimes they would respond with abusive indignation. They took any opportunity they could to attack both the thoughts and the very person who shared these thoughts. They did so with a barrage of words and actions that made heads spin for those involved and even some of those who observed.

The fallout of their negative behavior degraded many opportunities for harmonious discourse. They employed dissention with every word they conveyed. Their mere presence would be a signal to shut discourse down. Many left who came together for intelligent exchange. They soon shut down any efforts to share Light contrary to what they dogmatically held to be true.

It was clear to all of us that the Light we shared was not welcome by Darkness.

Further Down the Path

As thoughts evolved around the differences between Freemasonry and Masonry, investigations continued. Thoughts were exchanged and conclusions became more refined. Other premises that were normally taken for granted, were approached, inspected and ascertained as to whether they could be taken to be valid any longer. A whole new world of investigation soon unfolded before our eyes.

We each traveled down our own Freemasonic rabbit holes spelunking across the unwieldy gaps. We crossed the deep abysses that previous conjectures wrought by other Travelers. We unraveled their maps and cleared the rubbish left by untempered and overzealous imaginings. We fearlessly faced the dogmatic guard dogs that so often block the paths that should be sought by every dedicated Brother. We held tight to the belief that there was more to what was offered than the superficial trappings that so many accept as the whole.

And we were delighted by what we found!

II. Confusion in the Temple

*When you want to know where to start to
unravel the Mysteries behind the Craft, Start by
Focusing upon the Blatant and Blaring
Misunderstandings and Inconsistencies that its
Membership Actively Refuses to Deal with Effectively*

When you remain even loosely active in Craft activities and have taken the time to discuss it at length and in depth with others, you shall soon become acutely aware that there are many aspects of the Craft that appear to be confusing at best, and deeply disconcerting at worst. These aspects shall continue to plague the Craft until such time that all members find themselves harmoniously discussing differences.

It was only after a few years within the Craft that I began comparing notes with my Brothers. It was not an easy task either. As you might know from your own experience, trying to come to a common understanding of things about the Craft even at a superficial level is sometimes blocked by many assumptions. After many misunderstandings and miscommunications I slowly became aware that I had to create a super-flexible translator for myself, especially when I tried to speak about the Craft with others.

Misunderstandings

There are many times when Brothers make an effort to draw distinctions between things that they are told and things that they observe. I became aware of this when I started reading and hearing key differentiating words inserted into conversations and discourses. This occurred most often when Brothers were describing who they saw and what they were doing.

The words that were used by them to distinguish some members from others were prefaced with *"True"*, *"Authentic"* and *"Real" as* opposed to *"False"*, *"Fake"* and *"Bogus"*. The words that followed these precursors were usually *"Brothers"*, *"Masons"*, *"Masonry"*, *"Freemasons"* and *"Freemasonry"*. In a very genuine way, each was making a sincere effort to communicate to others what they were seeing before them.

And this effort was not limited to members of the Craft. Writers who were not members of the Society used these very same methods to communicate that there were huge differences between members of the Society and those who actually Practiced the Principles that the Society espoused.

With more time and interactions, I became aware that there were Brothers who didn't use such prefacing words in their efforts to share what they saw. They opted for using words that were familiar to all but assigned, through their use, distinct meanings that would be understood by those who would read them.

Examples of this can be found within Craft writings throughout the 1800s and 1900s. There are countless times when the word *"Freemason"* was used by some authors to indicate members of the Craft who actually practiced the principles of the Society. These same writers would call other members who did not practice Societal Principles mere *"Masons"*. It was clear that their efforts were put forth to draw distinctions between two classes of members within the Society.

This caused tremendous confusion within those members who saw being a member synonymous with being a Freemason. They earnestly believed that if you are a member, you are both a Freemason and a Mason. The spotlights shown by authors upon members who were true to Society Principles and members who were untrue to these principles could not be seen by these Brothers. Because they could not see any difference, the main intents of the writers and speakers were utterly lost in the minutia of the confusing discourse.

Uncommon Ground

Adding to this situation is a clear reversal of meanings conveyed by some twenty-first century Brothers. They have summarily dismissed these conventions and adopted pre-Society distinctions that would appear to be a complete antithesis of these definitions. By taking the issue of practice outside the Society and assigning it strictly to practice versus non-practice, these Brothers have assigned a distinction that removes membership from the equation defining Masons. They have opted to define Freemasons as mere members of the Society of Free & Accepted Masons while in the same effort defining Masons as individuals who Practiced Principles that transform males toward maturity and wisdom regardless of affiliation.

In the eyes of some, Freemasons were members of a Society whereas Masons were Builders.

None of these definitions denoted that there was mutual exclusivity between the two. They didn't mean that members could not be Builders too or that Builders could not be members. It merely communicated a base understanding that one was not necessarily the other and one didn't have to be one to be the other.

Using this assignment of meaning and applying it to questions about historical figures can cause tremendous confusion within those not knowing these definitions. One such example is President Thomas Jefferson. It is quite clear that this man Raised himself up from Youth to Manhood and to Age. It is clear that he was not only mature but also wise in what he did with his time and efforts. It was also abundantly clear that he was a Builder of himself, his fellow men and the country which he helped found. He was also surrounded by men who were members of the Freemasonic Society. From all outward signs, this man was clearly a Mason (Builder) according to one set of assigned meanings. By another set of assigned meanings, what was not clear from anything that was written down about him was whether he was a member of the Society of Free & Accepted Masons and hence a Freemason (a Member of the Society).

Resistance

One of the biggest problems that differing definitions bring to Craft discourse is the unwillingness of certain members to accept that word meaning is assigned within the context of the communication. Furthermore, these same members have also steadfastly refused to accept that meaning does change in ways that may be counter to what they have come to understand and accept as true for themselves.

When listening to and reading discourse and debate between Society members, you can quickly pick up on those who grasp this understanding and who stubbornly refuse to accept the offered meanings in any way. Within a very short time, the discourses involving these men degrade to arguments of definitions rather than the actual intent of the person trying to communicate Light. Rather than trying to seek to first understand[12] what the other person is trying to communicate, the effort is put forth by these listeners to have the person accept the listener's well-entrenched meanings before further discourse can occur.

As a result of listener resistance, many possibly valuable communications end in battles over what definitions are right and wrong rather than trying to get past these superficial labels and into the meat and bone of what is trying to be communicated. Such discourses also tend to eventually degrade into personal attacks upon the persons offering the Light by those who dogmatically oppose how this Light is offered.

Many members believe that this condition within the Craft shall not change anytime soon. It is part and parcel of what occurs when the Society itself refuses to educate its members along the lines of what is professed through its Rituals. As long as members are allowed to Progress in name only, that is, reciting back what they are told rather than thinking deeply about, understanding, and applying what they are told, such Craft disconnects between societal members shall continue.

Inconsistencies

The meanings that members assign to Craft words are not the only wide variables that you shall find within the Society. A huge inconsistency that many members see and experience is between what is spoken of within Craft Ritual and what is expected of them from the actual organization. Given any one specific arena of encounters among members of the Craft, you shall see that there is a higher than usual probability that several members shall display character that is utterly counter to that which is espoused by Societal Ritual.

One such inconsistency is the support one would normally expect from an organization that espouses at every turn that they are about transforming good men into Better men. This is stated upfront and is supported by words and phrases sprinkled throughout the entirety of its Rituals, Lectures, Laws and other Organizational writings. For an organization that professes so highly the value of Bettering men, the stark desert of support its members see before them and the experience they have as a result of their participation, leaves many disenchanted by the words that fall sweetly upon their eager ears.

Problems that arise as a result are plentiful. One involves the literal translation of what is shared within

Ritual. This occurs even though it is readily apparent, or should be from what Freemasonic writings share, that Ritual is Allegorical and Symbolic. Even with this being stated, there are many within the Society that make every effort to understand, convey and live Ritual as if it were not Allegorical and Symbolic.

This becomes clear when you see the activities that members engage in surrounding their investigation of elements found within the third Degree drama. This includes either what they experienced directly or of what they are informed, depending upon how their Jurisdiction goes about it. Some members take the Dramatic information and experience as if it were some secret history that is being kept hidden from the world. Others believe there is an actual Lost Word. Still others believe the story conveyed is more accurate than the Scriptures it was based upon.

All things considered, with even minor Perpending, it should become clear that such fanciful flights of imagination would be better guided if the Society as a whole helped its members do the Work that its Rituals direct men toward. This would be preferred behavior. Instead, the present Society merely assures that Candidates experience the Ritual as required. They soon wear titles that don't truly represent what they originally did within the Stonecraft Society from which they were supposedly taken.

Erosion

Between the misunderstanding and inconsistencies lie a perpetual production of disillusionment and disappointment within members who eagerly joined the Craft. Candidates Entering the Society usually have high hopes of being surrounded by men who have actually developed Life Masteries. What they find is a wide assortment of males who have yet to master themselves, much less the principles of the Craft. They also find men obsessed with memorizing things that they have no desire to understand, much less apply. Included in this are statements from these very men that continually encourage similar attitudes and behaviors within new members who obviously want more from their investment of money, time and energy.

With no true leadership or examples of what the Society can actually do to develop good men into Better men, some members soon realize that the organization is not what they expected. Couple this with meetings that provide little to no nourishment for those who attend, it becomes very clear to any man who was initially excited about joining the Society, that it offers little more than activities that maintain the process of Initiating men three times over.

Many men leave the Society soon thereafter, believing they have obtained all that the Society has to offer. Other men continue to be dues paying members. They are still motivated enough to continue having a connection with the Craft but rarely if ever attend meetings. They realize too soon that meetings offer nothing of interest to them. A fewer number of members continue to maintain the process, believing it offers worthwhile activities to engage in, regardless of expectations truly never being met.

III. Comparing the Crafts

*It should be abundantly clear that
Stonemasonry and Freemasonry are
nowhere near the same.*

When seeking to understand Freemasonic roots, it is important to examine its assumptions and premises. Examining those roots attributed to Stonemasons reveals that we might not have as much in

common as is almost universally accepted within the Organization of Freemasons. A side by side comparison of Stonemasonry and Freemasonry reveals very quickly that they are not the same thing. Even when you superimpose their separate attributes upon the Operative-Speculative claims, it should be evident that the metaphors of each practice break down rapidly.

Let's take a close look at each.

Stonemasonry (Stonecraft)

Stonemasons, referred to as *Operative Masons* by Freemasonic Society members, have been around since the time when men first took tool to stone. The materials they crafted came from the earth and were hewn into whatever shapes suited their purposes. The materials by virtue of their nature were long-lasting. Stonecrafters are responsible for monuments, temples, cathedrals, artifacts, statues, cities, roads, walls, dams and an assortment of other edifices found around the globe.

In years past, membership in a Society of Stonemasons allowed for many benefits associated with the trade and employment.

Freemasonry (The Craft)

Freemasons, also referred to as *Speculative Mason* by Freemasonic Society members, have been around since the beginning of the Grand Lodge Era, and perhaps had their quickening in the activities that brought about this Era. The materials Freemasons claim to work are supposed to be Spiritual in nature. Freemasons are responsible for preserving the Degrees that they experienced when they joined and through which they progressed. Some of them are also responsible for providing the same exact words and manners to those who also join after them, but this is an auxiliary responsibility that only some accept. All members take upon themselves Obligations that are part of each Degree experienced. Various members have started other auxiliary Organizations for charitable purposes, but these are the only things that have been built, other than more Lodges and Grand Lodges. Their buildings and charities are found around the world.

It is often confused with *Free Masonry,* which is *Excellent or Superior Building* that originally focused upon Stonecraft alone.[13] Freemasonry is a Society that focuses almost exclusively upon the Initiation of men into their Society for the purpose of integrating them into Lodge Activities. This is often referred to as "Making Masons"

Membership in the Freemasonic Society allows for rights, benefits and information associated with Freemasonic Lodges and Grand Lodges that are Recognized by each member's Jurisdiction. All these allowances relate directly back to the Organization itself.

Stonemasonry Defined

Stonemasonry *"is the craft of shaping rough pieces of rock into accurate geometrical shapes, at times simple, but some of considerable complexity, and then arranging the resulting stones, often together with mortar, to form structures."* [14]

Freemasonry Defined

If we were to take the previous definition and apply it metaphorically to Freemasonry and with some minor adjustments, we would have something similar and in line with an assumed origin. Freemasonry is the craft of shaping rough men into smoother men, at times simple, but often of considerable complexity, and then arranging the resulting men, often together with the cement of Brotherly love and affection, to form various organizational structures.

But to say any of this would be forcing the metaphor since there are virtually no supported activities within existing Society structures to do any of what is stated. Organizational structures already exist and members are merely instructed as to how the Organization desires them to fit in, support those structures and possibly replicate them.

Stonemasons

When examining how stonemasons are classified, we find that there are several types. It is an assembly line of activities of which each type engages and makes possible the activities of the next. It all starts at the Quarries.

The *Quarrymen* split veins, or sheets of rock, and extract the resulting blocks of stone from the ground.[15]

The *Sawyers* cut these rough blocks into cuboids, to required size with diamond-tipped saws. [16]

There are *Banker* masons who are workshop based. They specialize in working the stones into the shapes required by a building's design. The Banker mason's tools, methods and skill sets have existed as a trade for thousands of years.[17]

The *Carvers* cross the line from craft to art. They use their artistic ability to carve stone into foliage, figures, animals or abstract designs.[18]

Fixer masons specialize in the fixing of stones onto buildings. They use lifting tackle, and traditional lime

 mortars and grouts to affix stones. Sometimes modern cements, mastics and epoxy resins are also used. [19]

Memorial masons or *monumental* masons carve gravestones and inscriptions.[20]

Each of these masons might be involved in any one or all of the following types of Stonemasonry: Rubble Masonry[a], Ashlar Masonry[b], Stone Veneer Masonry[c], or Slipform Masonry[d], depending upon the need and their training.

Freemasons

When examining how Freemasons are classified, we find there are several types. They too have an assembly line of activities in which each type engages and makes possible the activities of the next. It all starts in the quarries too.

Unlike within Stonemasonry, the quarries Freemasons work are those involving relationships with others. This is their quarry and any gathering is done only to those who have already freed themselves of obligations that would prevent them from being considered for membership. In this respect Freemasonic Quarrymen do not extricate. They merely identify those who have already extracted themselves and seek to join the Craft.

If we were to continue to seek and see parallels to Stonemasonry, the Freemasonic Sawyer would be responsible for assuring that the quarried individual called *a Petitioner* was properly assessed and prequalified for both Acceptance into the Society and Admittance into the Lodge.[21] Once the Petitioner is inspected and voted on for both Acceptance into the society and Admittance into the Lodge, he is then referred to as a *Candidate*.

---

[a] roughly dressed stones are laid in a mortar
[b] finely dressed (cut, worked) stonework
[c] protective and decorative cover stonework for interior or exterior walls and surfaces
[d] building stone walls with the aid of formwork

After the Candidate is Accepted and Admitted by going through the first Degree, he is told that he is responsible for shaping himself. Often no such activity is actually undertaken by the Candidate with any certainty or Society support. Even though each is self-responsible, the Lodge does make effort to shape him toward Organizational needs with the use of a Freemasonic Banker.

This Banker is almost always a Coach, Mentor, Instructor or Tutor that assists the Candidate in memorizing up to three specific things before he is allowed to progress from one level to the next. Those things are part of an overall Proficiency that may or may not include all three elements, depending upon the Jurisdiction. Full Proficiencies usually include Inquiries and Responses that cover what occurred during any one Degree. Lesser Proficiencies might include just the Obligations stated within each Degree. Bare minimum Proficiencies just require the words, signs and grips that each Degree reveals to Candidate that he must use as Modes of Recognition.

When Candidates go through all three Degrees and wish to participate in Lodge activities as Officers or Degree Team members, Freemasonic Carvers are employed to help further shape these members into the specialties in which they want to engage.

If we were to push the metaphor further, Freemasonic Fixers are responsible for assuring that the superficial aspects of the Organization are taken care of well enough so that its image always comes across as professional to anyone viewing it.

If we were to include in this Memorial and Monumental Freemasons, we might want to associate them with the secretaries and press agents of the Organization.

Although parallels exist, the very core of what the two supports differs tremendously.

Stonecraft Apprenticeships

In medieval times, the starting age of Apprenticeship was just prior to puberty. During his time of Apprenticeship, he would transform himself physically from a youth to an adult, all while learning the Craft and learning about what it is to be a man, especially one that knows the trade.

A Candidate for Apprenticeship of this era was to be unbound, having no other obligations that would prevent him from binding himself to the Craft. He would do so for a total of Seven years before he would be permitted to enjoy the Freedoms of the Craft.

Apprentices were required to engage in activities that developed them and because they did so for seven years, they also developed relationships and the skills those relationships required.

The Stonemasons of medieval times traditionally and contractually served apprenticeships of seven years before being allowed to work as journeyman. Systems requiring and offering Stonemasonry apprenticeships are still in

operation to this day, however they are more likely to last only three years rather than seven.

The time compression relates

mostly to the later age of those who enter into the profession coupled with advanced learning systems that employ hands-on experience and college style learning.

Building, hewing and theory are all a part of a comprehensive education. Along with manual skill development, there are also drafting work, blueprint reading, and sometimes construction conservation. During this time, familiarity with heights, hands on work, classroom learning and field work are all shaping the future of the worker.

Freemasonic Apprenticeships

To join the Society and receive the first Degree, Freemasonic Apprentices must be adults somewhere between the age of eighteen to twenty-five and above (depending upon Jurisdictional requirements). It is assumed by many within the Fraternity that this age range allows new members to be mature enough to grasp the lessons given them. This requirement is in direct conflict with ancient Stonecraft where mentors accepted underage males to enter into apprenticeships so that they can cultivate maturity into them. Of course, this too has changed from ancient times due to modern culture and education coupled with child labor laws.

In Freemasonry, there is no actual trade training related to Stonecraft, even when applied metaphorically. The Freemasonic Apprentice is not required to engage in any hands on work having to do with developing his ability to shape himself as a living stone. His only classroom work involves at best, memorizing and *"giving back"* what occurred during his Degrees. This activity includes reciting specific words and gestures that are provided by a trainer. More extensive requirements might include repeating back specific Obligations and responses to specific Inquiries.

Each stage of Progression, called comprehensively *Degree work* is typically relegated to thirty day intervals before the next Degree can be experienced, but even this time varies depending upon the Jurisdiction.

Expressing Progression

Of course, even this is not required in some Jurisdictions when a Grand Lodge waves the usual requirements and allowed Lodges to have what are called *One Day Classes*. Such *"short form"* events dismiss all the usual training requirements of all three Degrees allowing Profanes[22] to gain entitlement to all the Rights, Lights and Benefits of membership within hours. No Work is involved; just participation.

There are a few advantages according to some advocates of these events. Foregoing the usually required training allows the sponsoring Lodge to reap huge financial benefits from those who go through the Degrees. It brings in dues paying members in high numbers, something that helps boost the coffers of both Lodges and Grand Lodges. Furthermore, if we go by what is typically shared by short form advocates, the time compression of one day is found to bring in long term membership support equal to that which is obtained by those who go through the more lengthy Progression.

The downside of such events is that the time compression short-circuits development of Fraternal relationships, development of Freemasonic knowledge and skill-sets. It also robs the Candidates of the traditional path that previous members experience working their way through each Degree.

The ramifications of this short-circuiting are huge. New One Day Class members do not have time to adjust to Fraternal life. They do not have the usual time to develop a rich history with existing members. They don't have the experience of investing in learning about the Fraternity and the Craft that the Society practices. They are unlikely to enter a Lodge unaided and participate in Lodge activities, be it Degree work or business meetings.

In effect, short form members are Brothers in name and title only for they have no strong Foundation supporting either. They are lost if they show up at all. They have not served a necessary time in training to properly prepare themselves to participate as informed members.

Stonecraft Fellow Crafts and Masters

At one point in time in the Middle Ages, it took seven years to earn the right to be a Journeyman, otherwise known as a Fellow in the Craft. After being bound to a mentor who had himself earned the right, and proving that, as an Apprentice, he had indeed learned the Craft as was taught to him by his teacher, he would then be allowed to work freely within the trade.

Masters were themselves Journeyman who had, after years of work, earned the right to be called *a Master*. This included creating a Masterpiece that other Masters recognized as such. Additional to this, they had put enough financial support or had obtained financial backing to open a Lodge for the purposes of commencing a project.

Freemasonic Fellow Craft and Masters

For an Apprentice to become a Fellow Craft within the Freemasonic Order, no skill development or servitude under a mentor is required. Memorization of words, signs and grips are almost universally required. Some Apprentices are required to know the Obligations they learned during their first Degree. A few are even required to do all this and also recite what occurred to them during their Degree.

When you don't include what occurs within the One Day Classes, the waiting period between Degrees varies from one Jurisdiction to another from anywhere between one month to six typically, with some Jurisdiction requiring a year or more.

After proving himself Proficient in what was just described, and waiting until a designated period of time had elapsed, the Apprentice is then permitted to receive his Fellow Craft Degree.

Likewise, to obtain the Master's title, the Fellow Craft does the same as the Apprentice but for the second Degree materials. No Mastery is required of him other than reciting back words, signs and grips that he is provided.

The Big Question

There are quite a few major differences between Stonecraft and Freemasonry. Even if you take the premise that Freemasonry was started by Stonecraft Brothers, the metaphor of Operative to Speculative work breaks down very quickly when you apply it to what is truly supported by our current Freemasonic Organizations. Quality control alone shows that what is professed to be important is not systematically supported in any manner, unless a Regulation or Obligation is being violated to the point where it reflects poorly upon the Organization. No cultivation or development of Betterment of Men is deliberately focused upon or consciously exercised as an Organizational activity.

Unlike Stonecraft, Freemasonic Members are not required to craft anything real or imaginary under the canopy of heaven. They are provided an Instruction Set in the form of Ritual as to what they should do to become

Better men but they are provided no support to assure that they learn how to become Better men. They are only required to memorize that Instruction Set, not Execute it. That is the only activity that they are required to do to prove that they have become Proficient in the "Craft" at any specific level up to the third. No further Proficiencies are required. Furthermore, understanding this provided instruction set is not required or supported by the majority of members.

The only other membership requirement to which they commit is assuring that they conform as members to the existing Organizational structures. No Innovative activities are permitted to the existing body of predefined Freemasonic works.

It is clear that this activity and their limits do not support Freemasonic Craft in being a Progressive Science, only a stagnant script to follow that very few members if any understand.

There are a host of other noticeable differing aspects that can also be gleaned very quickly by observation and comparison. Much could be said, but the point would not be any more made. What is clear though is that any intelligent man who takes it upon himself to perform even the most rudimentary examination of Freemasonry would soon discover for himself that it has as much in common with Stonecraft as Spirit has with Stone.

That being said, if Freemasonry is indeed not a continuation of or a metaphorical application of Stonecraft, what actual Craft is it?

IV. Describing Today's Craft

No matter how many ways you may want to Prescribe what the Craft ought to be, when you don't take the time to Observe its actual Operations and accurately Describe it, you Participate in a Projected Illusion and not an Engaged in Reality.

It was very shortly after I had become a full member of the Freemasonic Society when I began looking around at its actual workings. I don't mean to say that it was the Ritual work that I examined. It was the actual functioning of the Organization itself on which I focused.

It's not unusual for me to engage in this type of activity when I am involved within an organization. My profession is that of a Business Coach. Business Coaches are trained to understand the current operation of an organization and make recommendations as to how things could be done more effectively. In this respect, I'm hired by top level decision makers to examine how organizations function with the intent to bring about much better effectiveness of operation.

As you might imagine, this training could lead to quite a few disturbing moments when examining a volunteer organization such as the Fraternity.

Upon First Examination

What I found were the typical things that you would find in many volunteer organizations that have few or no paid members. There are always more things to do than people to do them. There are always shortfalls of time, money and man-power and it is the central focus of many business meetings. The Quantity versus Quality discussion is forever debated with most efforts to solve or resolve issues being heavily biased toward addressing the symptoms and not the cause of the troubles. The presumed purpose of the Organization always takes a backseat to the actual purpose and it is always reframed to look like the actual purpose is supporting the presumed.

Let's take a close look at the premises shared with many Brothers through Organizational Operations, Ritual, Lectures, Laws, Oral Traditions and General Propaganda.

Premises

1. **Origins** – It is assumed that the Organization as a whole is a continuation of an organization that was started in time immemorial[23].
2. **Crisis** – It is assumed that at one point the very product of the Organization was no longer in high enough demand to maintain enough income to keep the Organization sustainable.
3. **Conversion** – It is assumed that the product focus changed from Building Physical Stone Edifices and the like to Edifices that are spiritual and non-physical in nature.
4. **Unaltered** – It is assumed that the Rituals that have been passed down from mouth to ear and from one man to the next have been the same since Time Immemorial.

5. **Preservation** – It is assumed that all members shall do everything within their limitations to assist in the Preservation and Dissemination of Ritual, Tenets and Principles of Freemasonry.

6. **Participation** – It is assumed that all members shall participate in Lodge activities based upon their personal limitations.

7. **Mastery** – It is assumed that every member can and should achieve Mastery by applying himself.

Let's take a closer look at each of these premises.

Origins

If you are like most in the Craft who have been around for any length of time, you have most likely heard or read at least a half dozen or so theories as to the Origins of the Craft. You might have read that it started sometime during the middle ages with Stonemasons. If you include the whole implemented concept of Grand Lodges, you might have come across a theory that discloses origins of the first Grand Lodge and associates it solely with the York Rite though association with King Athelstan[24] in and around 926 CE. You might have also read that the Craft truly started in 1356 CE with a demarcation dispute that brought about the creation of trade regulation in London England. Another theory you might have read was that it started in Ancient Rome or even further back in Ancient Greece. One author put forth that it started in Egypt and then goes into the how, why, and when. Yet another theory has it that it was here in the beginning with the creation and teaching of Adam.

Each theory is impressive for a variety of reasons, both positive and negative. Each theory appeals to a specific cross-section of members, depending on who reads it and his interests. Each has a plethora of information supporting the multiple premises, arguments and conclusions of each author, supporting each theory in their own special way. Each leads the readers down roads of adventure filled with an abundance of facts and follies.

Yet, no matter what you might have already read about Craft origins, the fact remains that each of these theories focuses upon the origins of the wrong Craft! The authors have all misled themselves and hence their readers. The theories have each been put forth with premises that are not themselves supportive of the actual Craft.

And each theory, being off the mark, has misled generations of men down the wrong roads of discovery and for all the wrong reasons.

Were any of these theories actually correct? Did any one of them actually come close to reality? As we continue down this road, it should eventually become clear as to why these theories were put forth and why they all missed the point.

Crisis

We are led to believe that there was a crisis faced by the Stoneworker guilds sometime before the start of Grand Lodge Era (~1717 CE). The Stoneworkers were getting less and less business and, as a result, they were losing membership due to the changing times and economy.

(I shall take a moment and pause here so that the significance of this statement sinks in. I hope that you do not miss the opportunity to overlay this past reality with what is occurring in our Craft today.)

Supposedly, there was a genuine fear that what had been found would be lost forever and what was found was something very special that should be preserved.

This premise sounds pretty neatly tied up save for a few facts that tend to dismiss this premise quickly.

First off, there was no crisis. Economies continually shift and workers must continually find work elsewhere either in the same field or another one that shall pay. Lodges were convened when there was work to be done and pay to be paid. When either one or the other ceased to exist, Lodges folded and workmen scattered to find work and pay elsewhere. This was a common occurrence.

Secondly, Lodge membership was always temporary even when you were a member of a town or city guild. Lodges themselves convened for Work. They generally disbanded once work or pay ran out.

Thirdly, there was nothing that was found that any one Lodge protected other than its own trade secrets. There are no trade secrets that had any value in a changing economy. In such an economy, trade secrets no longer had any value since there was little to no work to use them, *unless they could be used elsewhere.*

Was there ever any crisis? Was anything that actually occurred to drive Lodges toward what ultimate arose as a presumed response? It should become clear that no such crisis existed, but it made for a great and compelling metaphor.

Conversion

The premise of conversion goes like this: *Faced with the crisis of lowered demand for both product and skilled laborers, the loss of Lodge members and the need to preserve what was found (namely the trade itself), four Lodges came together and formed a Grand Lodge to standardize Ritual Practices and to allow non-operative members to join with the clear intent of having them become the Preservationists of the Stoneworker's Traditions and Rituals.*

The new members were eventually called *Speculative Masons* to highlight the fact that they were not Stoneworkers in the material sense. They were to metaphorically work upon spiritual temples, houses not made by hand, and they have supposedly done so ever since.

The conversion from Operative to Speculative occurred within most every Lodge associated with the Premier Grand Lodge and has been this way ever since.

On first inspection, the provided conversion premise sounds like an awesome idea. Just convert over what the Stonemasons did to what Speculative Masons can do. It should be simple enough, yet a problem arises very quickly upon inspection.

First of all, Stonemasons built things. Secondly, they served apprenticeships that required specific skill development that enabled them to become skilled tradesmen. Thirdly, they joined the Stonemason Society so that they may join Lodges when work and payment were available for the trade that they offered in return.

Speculative Masons do not build things. They join the Society when they join a Lodge, they pay for the right to be part of that Lodge and they do not ply any trade in exchange for fee. Although there is a widely circulated quote by Brother Benjamin Franklin as to the wages a Brother can expect, it is not for building anything other than relationships, if that.

Unaltered

Freemasonic instruction inculcates that the Ritual that men experience remains unaltered since Time Immemorial. This is one of the main reasons offered for all the archaic words, phrases and manners used within it. Another reason offered, is highlighted in one of the Freemasonic Landmarks that some USA Jurisdictions recognize in their Constitutions.

The Landmark states:

That the landmarks of Masonry can never be changed. These constitute the landmarks, or as they have sometimes been called, "the body of Masonry," in which it is not in the power of man or a body of men to make the least innovation.

Between the two, we are left to believe that Freemasonry's Rituals haven't been altered and there is a proscription stating that it shall not be altered, especially if you accept that to alter anything is to innovate it.

Upon further inspection we find that things are not quite that way. Rituals around the globe and within the USA, from one Jurisdiction to the next, are clearly not the same. They are altered and in some instances hardly recognizable in the case of non- Preston-Webb based Ritual. When pressed further, we come to find that when new Grand Lodges were formed, they borrowed bits and pieces from a variety of Rituals, adding, adjusting and modifying them to make them unique unto that Jurisdiction.

So that it is very clear what is being said here and there is no question as to the intent, these actions are clearly *Innovations* to Ritual and are contrary to the very words communicated to Candidates progressing through the Degrees and to those members expected to adhere to these words without wavering.

The premise of Landmarks or Ritual being unaltered is false.

Preservation

Members are continuously enrolled into Preservation activities. In many USA Jurisdictions, the central preservation task they are encouraged to do is preserve the

Ritual. They do this by memorizing what they experienced during their Degree. This is called *Proficiencies.*

Typical Proficiencies that are still fully practiced are a series of Inquiries and Responses that are exchanged between a Catechist and a Catechumen. Lengthy Proficiencies also include specific Obligations that a member willingly takes upon himself and specific consequences that he shall knowingly suffer as a result of not honoring those responsibilities. Lastly, these types of Proficiencies include explicit gestures that have special and specific significance to Brothers who have also experienced the Degree. All these efforts are put forth in the spirit of Progression and it is required in many USA Jurisdictions for advancement to occur.

The premise of this activity is to preserve from "mouth to ear" what has been handed down this way from one man to another since Time Immemorial. Simple research shows that this technique is not universally used. Many Jurisdictions do not require any such memorization other than what is referred to as "The Modes of Recognition". Since the entirety of Ritual, Lectures and associated Choreography are written down and preserved by the Grand Lodge in each Jurisdiction, it is easily seen that there are other reasons that are more valid for this activity than simply trying to preserve what is handed down from Mouth to Ear.

What are the true reasons for this activity? Why is so much time spent upon it in some Jurisdictions and not others? As we progress in our evaluation, it shall become abundantly clear.

Participation

There is a continuous hum and often times a whine that is heard in almost all Jurisdictions within the USA. That noise is generated by the members of those Lodges and is acutely focused upon having members attend their functions. This noisy chatter is not isolated to the Lodges within USA Jurisdictions. It can be heard also around the globe and is generated by the multitude of Lodges who all suffer from what is presumed to be a lack of membership attendance.

Although it is true that membership attendance is lacking in far too many Lodges, it is assumed that bringing members back shall clear up this annoying and irritating condition.

This assumption though is clearly wrong. Lack of attendance is a symptomatic trouble caused by much bigger problems. As long as any one Lodge focuses its efforts upon working upon solving a symptomatic trouble, it shall continuously face the trouble because the problem is never addressed.

First off, the premise of Lodge attendance is flawed, misleading and unsupported. The very nature of Ritual's goal is to create Traveling men who are self-sufficient, self-reliant and self-regulated. You cannot expect to bring such men into being and then have them remain due to some misguided belief that they are not good Brothers unless they attend Lodge functions. Guilt trips don't work on mature men wanting more from their life investment.

Secondly, to be convincing you must properly assess the reasons men have for joining the Society and clearly determine that these reasons were to attend Lodge functions that supported those reasons. Unless you do, you can't reasonably expect members to attend Lodge activities if the reasons they joined don't support attendance.

Thirdly, if you don't provide to members membership activities that are in line with the excitement and drama that interested them in the beginning, you're likely to lose them fairly quickly after they realize there's nothing more for them.

The premise of Lodge attendance echoes the premise of the Crisis and neither of them has been truly validated by the actions taken to deal with the presumed problem of lack of attendance.

Current Craft activities are not designed to keep the interest of men who are seeking intellectually stimulating environments. One might conclude these activities may be designed to actually drive such men away.

What can be done to change things so that Lodge activities are more attractive to such men? What needs to be added to the current Blue Lodge offerings? Perhaps nothing at all needs to change. Perhaps the Blue Lodge experience is perfectly designed to get the results it gets and its more active members have been misled by unknowing mentors into believing these results aren't okay.

Mastery

The premise of Mastery is sweet to the ears of so many who are attracted to the Society. There are many who join with the expressed intent of attaining Mastery. This intention is exactly the end goal that one would conclude from the Progression that occurs within the Blue Lodge experience.

But do the expressed goals of achieving Mastery match with the actual support provided by the Organization and those running it? Do all the activities truly develop and cultivate Mastery within those individuals labeled Master Masons?

Let's take a close look at what Organizational activities are required to bring a man to eventually wear the Organizational title of *"Master"*.

1) *Experiencing three Recognized Degrees in a Recognized Lodge.*
2) *Memorizing and repeating back what one was told to say and do afterward.*

3) *Keeping current on paying Dues.*
4) *Showing no outward signs of what others could perceive
    to be immorality.*

That's it. There is nothing more required of any member other than doing these listed items. There is absolutely no requirement to actually do anything that each Degree says or recommends be done. There are no officially sanctioned activities by any Grand Lodges offered through their Lodges that assists Brothers to do anything other than Proficiencies that are approved by the Jurisdiction's Grand Lodge.

So what Mastery is actually being developed as a consequence of participating in the offered and supported activities of the Lodge? This question and all that is implied by it brought about a Craft revelation for me. It was an implication that had been clearly overlooked by all those who sought to find Craft origins. What's more, from all outward signs, it had been overlooked from the very beginning.

This, in relation to all the other premises reviewed herein, clarified for me that the origins that have been mentioned had clearly missed their mark.

So Many Questions

From the start, it was very clear that some of my Brothers and I were unsatisfied by the responses we received to some very important questions. These questions related to the Organization's Origin, its Operation and its Purpose. All of the responses seemed to be legitimate but upon closer examination appeared to conflict with known facts and observations.

The Origin question, no matter how it was asked, always remained unsatisfactorily answered. No matter what the answer, it was always some sort of mishmash of history that was loosely connected and filled with conjectures. All of which didn't seem to match up with what we observed occurring within the day to day operation of the Fraternity. There were clear disconnects that remained as ripped fabric flailing in the wind.

The Operation question was usually straightforwardly answered. Unfortunately, when the answer was lined up against what was espoused by Ritual, it too always seemed wanting. How we operate as an Organization, who we put in Positions and how we treat our Brothers all appear antagonistic to what we are supposed to be. The conflict between the two was very confusing.

Finally, there was the Organizational Purpose which, although was usually provided through slogans like *"Masonry makes good men better"* or descriptions like *"a peculiar system of morality, veiled in allegory, illustrated by symbols"* didn't quite match up with the legal description. Legal descriptions usually include statements attesting to the Organization being a *religious, educational and charitable* organization. It could be assumed that there are no inconsistencies in any of these since there are overlaps.

Although it espouses transformative education within its Rituals, it doesn't actually provide toward what Ritual points. Its education is all concentrated toward Performing Degrees or Lodge Operation. These are two extremely narrow educational focuses. Any educational effort made by members that tries to actually expand upon what is spoken of in Ritual is sporadic and wholly unsupported by the Organization, its many leaders and most of its general membership.

The religious nature of the Organization is also very narrow. It's explained by the membership having to believe in God or a Supreme Being. This along with all the

52

scriptural references used with Ritual, some generic prayers
to The Grand Architect of the Universe shared at specific
moments during Lodge activities and a Volume of Sacred
Law that must be opened upon the Altar. Other than these
three items, there are no further religious influences other
than the Morality, beliefs and attitudes men bring with
them into the Lodge experience.

As an aside, debates about whether Freemasonry is a
religion or not usually take place in small groups, on-line in
some cloistered Internet forum or in a publically accessible
website group. There are typically no winners in the debate
and it almost always ends with uncivil jabs between
participants who cannot come to some mutually satisfying
definition much less agreement.

All of which leaves many of the members scratching
their heads trying to make sense of the whole Organization.
The closer each member looks at it though, the more
questions always seem to come up, especially for those
who try to gain some form of clarity or traction. But when
you describe what is actually going on within the ranks, the
only thing that becomes obvious is that it is indeed a
charitable Society.

I confess that I was one of many who went looking
down this road, seeking more Light that seemed to be there.
I continued to look to see what I could find, in spite of the
frustrations I faced daily. I had some success, but not in the
directions I had originally thought I'd find them.

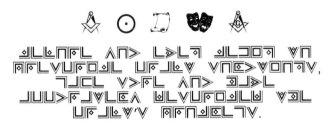

V. The Masterful Roots

When you Seek the Mysteries of Freemasonry, you had best be sure that what you seek is exactly what is being offered.

In my quest to uncover the true origins of the Craft, I came across a curious connection ferreting through some etymological materials. Interestingly enough, it was found looking up the word roots of *Mastery* and *Mystery*. At first, I put this connection aside while I pursued other seemingly more promising leads. At that time it was not what I thought that I was looking for. But I was mistaken and as fate would have it, this connection continued to harass me until I finally looked into it further. And I am very glad that I did.

Originally, my quest entailed seeking the roots of the word *Mastery*. What drove me? I was disturbed by what I had seen the word *Master* applied to within the Fraternity. By all outward appearances, it seemed as if the word was merely used as a superficial title that had little to nothing to do with Mastery. This was disturbing since one of the premises behind my joining the Society was to develop the very Mastery that was missing from my life and to which I earnestly believed the Fraternity would assist me in Developing and Cultivating. In effect, once I had joined and achieved *"Master"* status, I knew deep down below that Master's cloak that I was not what the cloak denoted.

So I sought a better understanding of the word and I believed looking into its etymology would reveal more about how it came to mean what it does today, especially within the Craft.

Upon further investigation, I found to my delight that the Word *Mastery* has the same roots as the word *Mystery*. They both meant at one time *"handicraft, trade, art"*, which came from another Medieval Latin root that meant *"service, occupation, office, ministry"* [25].

As it was originally used in the late fourteenth century, it reflected a man's trade, handicraft[26] or profession. At that time, it would not have been uncommon for a man to be asked what his *Mystery* was and to have him state his occupation. It should be no small wonder how the two words were intimately entwined as all trades had secrets that would be closely guarded and only shared with those who were worthy and could be trusted not to share them with outsiders, no matter what the situation.

The other meaning that the word *Mystery* relates to is what is now commonly accepted: that which is associated with *secrets, usually those involving rites, worship and hidden things.*

From the provided information it became clear to me that when you truly desire to learn the Mysteries of Freemasonry, you're going to have to study the Craft and make your efforts more than just a mere preoccupation to find secrets. It's no small Mystery! You're going to have to *become* exactly what you *Seek* and do so with *Mastery*.

But it also became clear that the provided etymological information was about to reveal the true gem that would eventually lead me to Freemasonry's origins.

That Intriguing Yet Annoying Footnote

It was while I continued to examine the roots of these two entangled words that I read something which tugged strongly at my curiosity. And I am delighted that it did. There, at the very end of all the descriptions and points made within the etymological data was the following seemingly innocent line:

> *"Now [the words "Mastery" and Mystery" are connected] only in **mystery play**, in reference to **the medieval performances, which often were staged by members of craft guilds.**"* [27]

This was an immensely interesting statement to me. I had not known that Craft Guilds put on such staged performances. Neither did I know that they were called *Mystery Plays.* Moreover, I had only a slight understanding as to what Mystery plays were and so I decided to investigate them further. And what I learned helped set the stage for a much better understanding of the roots of Freemasonry.

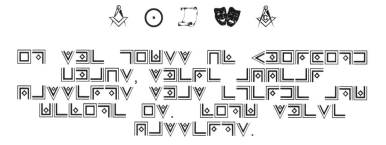

VI. The Mysteries

Mysteries: A Word on Plays.

Mastery begins when you Know that the answers you're Told are not Truly the Answers you Seek.

As I dug into the books, articles and associated website links having to do with Mystery plays, I quickly became overwhelmed with information related to the topic of interest. I was hoping to find further connections between them and our Craft today.

Trying to understand how Freemasonry came to be Practiced as it is this day was very important to me. *Why? What drove me?* I firmly believed that finding its true origins would give my Brothers and me insight into how the current day challenges faced by the Craft could be dealt with more effectively. As I have heard many times before:

> *"If you do not know where you come from, then you don't know where you are, and if you don't know where you are, then you don't know where you're going. And if you don't know where you're going, you're probably going wrong."* — *Terry Pratchett*

If many of the assumptions and premises made by Brothers over the last 300 years are wrong, then what we are doing as members to improve the Craft might actually be counterproductive. Furthermore, based upon the current decline of the Craft, it could be a fair conclusion that what we are currently doing *is just that!* Knowing the roots of the Craft would help guide us toward more fruitful actions and hopefully less frustration.

I believed that it is important to know the Craft's origins. So much has been written that simply did not fit with what was currently Practiced. Little did I know that to find this out would involve excavating deeply around the roots of its quarried theaters and more specifically, those of the Vernacular plays that evolved during the Middle Ages.

The Play's the Thing

Digging into the materials, I soon found that the plays in question were one of several Vernacular plays performed mostly during the Middle Ages. These plays evolved over time into three distinct forms, each of which had their special qualities.

Further burrowing revealed that all these forms had their roots in Liturgical plays which were put forth in the early Middle Ages in efforts to bring religious themes to a largely illiterate population. By about 925 CE, these efforts came to be known as Miracle (or Saint) plays[28].

The Bane is Banned

But, from what the research shows, it took some time for plays to get to this point.

Prior to circa 925 CE, religious influences all but closed down theatrical troupes and their productions. With the fall of Rome, most all productions in Western Europe were looked down upon and even banned because of their Roman influences and themes. Because of this, any theatrical production that was not based upon the accepted Religion of the time and area was intensely discouraged.

It took about 400 years before theatrical producers caught on that focusing upon the acceptable religious materials of the times would open the doors to theater for them and those that would willingly support them. Soon thereafter, the Church of the time began supporting and encouraging such plays to continue bringing its message to the masses. Spotlighting Saints at first, Miracle plays would soon become the center of Church supported plays.

It's a Miracle

Without a doubt, Miracle plays were known for their religious focus. They began as simple scripturally based tropes[29], but with much creativity, added props and creative elaboration, they eventually expanded to multiday productions in some areas.

They were used very effectively by the religious leaders to market their dogma to the illiterate and ignorant masses. They also became a victim of their own success because the very same ignorant and illiterate masses were used within the plays to stage them. This added a particular unexpected twist to the productions in that many of the actors used their spotlight to convey their own remarkably different brand of scripture. This coupled with amateur actors playing to the audience with materials that religious leaders found to be objectionable because it more often than not deviated from the prescribed dogma of the church. This eventually led them to rethink their support of these ventures.

By about 1200 CE, the Viking invasions had subsided. The rise of both towns and guilds occurred. The participation of religious leaders within these plays had become non-existent due to their desire to distance themselves from the amateurish and irreverent actors. Even Pope Innocent III issued a papal edict[30] forbidding clergy from acting on a public stage.

Vernacular text soon replaced Latin, breaking the bond between English and French productions[31]. Non-scriptural additions were also strategically placed within the plays, along with comic passages.

Eventually, Miracle plays were soon accompanied by an alternative form of mass entertainment.

The Mysteries

With the withdrawal of sponsorship and support from the religious leaders of the time, the guilds took over these plays. And with that takeover, the plays soon became known as Mystery plays, but not because they were filled with secret, unknown and unknowable concepts. It was because the word *Mystery* at that time referred to the fact that they were supported and performed by the *"Mysteries",* otherwise known as the *"Occupational Guilds"*.

The takeover also shifted the focused of these plays less upon miracles and more upon specific scriptural stories attuned to special and significant holidays or events. Included in each guild's choice of scripture was the ability of each to use their chosen story to advertise its wares to those who would sit still long enough to watch the clearly well-placed products within their plays.

Early Marketing

Yes, you did read this right. Each guild performance of these Mystery plays also was a form of marketing used to advertise its particular trade and wares. Scriptures were specifically chosen to highlight what they offered so that those who viewed them would be exposed to their offerings. It was the medieval equivalent of paid advertising for a show.

As the popularity of these plays increased, so did the interest of those city leaders who saw them as a way of generating moneys for their coffers. Cities encouraged Guilds to participate in the pageantry of any and all events. This allowed each guild's plays and associated wares to be spotlighted to the local population. This increased sales and along with this the tax revenues of the local government.

Their Costs

Plays were not cheap to put on. Expenses were always part of the production. To assure all assorted production expenses were dealt with accordingly, the guilds elected Pageant Masters annually and task them with the collection of funds, called *pageant silver,* from each of their respective guild members.

Each Pageant Master was a specific guild's Business Manager of all the plays performed by his guild during his year in office. He was in effect the guild's Impresario[32] who was in charge of all theatrical operations from assuring the proper financing to due form of the performance. This included obtaining funding for the plays from Patrons willing to support their production and collecting the pageant silver from each guild member when not enough could be obtained through charitable benefactors.

Strings

The benefactors of these performances did not always provide finances unconditionally. Sometimes they would request messages or themes to be woven into a performance. Other times they might request to either be part of the production themselves or have someone they knew be placed within the production as a condition of their continued patronage. Perhaps a request might be made to have product placement within the performance to draw attention to their wares. Financing these plays required some interesting negotiations that sometimes affected the production as a whole.

Pageant Masters were also empowered to impose a variety of fines depending upon the situation. Fines were levied upon any guild member who was slow in providing their fair share of play support. Also, although the actors and supporting staff were paid customary fees for their services, they too were fined for forgetting parts, for sloppily delivered performances or poor support in general.

Morality for All

By about 1400 CE, a distinct form of Vernacular plays had emerged out of the two previous types. It focused upon Morality and not Scripture. These plays deviated from past offerings specifically in its use of both Allegory and Symbols to convey Symbolically Moral concepts to the viewing audience rather than scriptural themes.

Morality plays, also known as *Moralities* (or *Morality* in singular form) flourished until about 1550 CE. At that time a perfect storm of economic and political change occurred. Protestant Reformation targeted

theaters whose central focus was religious. Affluent patrons began sponsoring plays. Professional Acting groups having the support of local patrons invested in local buildings to hold higher quality performances. Printing presses allowed for flyers to be used for more effective and consistent marketing. A revived interest in classical Roman and Greek culture directed itself toward influencing the literature and theater of the day.

All in all, the culture and economics of the time drove theatrical productions out of the hands of amateurs, and more specifically, away from the guilds and into the hands of paid professionals.

Coffin Nails

Miracle plays and Moralities were eventually condemned by the religious community. It was both the Romanists and

Protestants that ultimately caused the decline of Biblically based plays. The plays had become ineffective due to the hollowness of their performances. All religious feeling had become absent and performances became disgraceful and scandalous. They became conventionalized empty productions.

As one author[33] wrote:

"Both Romanists and Protestants ultimately frowned upon the mysteries, and denounced them for their childishness and coarseness. <u>*The guilds, which had once gladly given time and money for their preparation, now felt the yearly tax burden.*</u> *The cycle of sacred drama had run its course. In France, performances were forbidden during the latter part of the sixteenth century. In Spain and in Catholic Germany, as well as in Italy, they persisted somewhat longer. In England they were forbidden by Henry VIII, but were restored again for a brief time under Mary. There were few performances after 1600. The last York play was in 1597, the last Newcastle play in 1589. The Chester plays died out with the sixteenth century. The most important result of all this dramatic activity was perhaps the fostering of a love for the theater, and the shaping of native material into rough dramatic form."* [34]

Mind Your Manners

With the takeover of theater by professional actors, the themes and focus changed once again. Vernacular plays once again transformed, transitioned and evolved into something new. In the spirit of the times, theatrical productions moved away from religious themes and

64

Moralities to more secular dramas. These types of plays are often referred to as "Manners".

Masteries

It is clear that guilds were responsible for putting on many Mysteries and Moralities during the middle ages. *This activity was not limited to only one specific guild or trade group.* There were many guilds and trades involved and they all had their specific plays that highlighted their wares and talents in particular.

What is also clear is that with the decline of guild participation in these plays, the craft as it was applied toward Moralities stopped. At least, it stopped as publically held events.

To the Tomb

What is the connection between these guild plays and modern day Freemasonry? It should be clear by now that the very core of what Freemasonry does today are *privatized plays.* The Society built them by combining *Miracle and Moralities plays.* In other words, the *Mysteries* of Freemasonry *are these plays* and they are rightfully named.

At the core of the Blue Lodge experience and Lodge Culture are three specific privatized *Mystery plays. They* are called the *Entered Apprentice, Fellow Craft* and *Master Mason* Degrees. Both the York and Scottish Rites are also a series of staged privatized plays. They are exemplified in total by the York Rite and, in some Jurisdictions, the Scottish Rite.

VII. The Grand Undertaking

The Transformation from strict Stonecraft to strict Theater-craft took just under a century to complete, and its impact upon the stage of humanity would be Tremendous.

It is evident that the existing documents from around the time of the Premier Grand Lodge continually point to the fact that certain Stonecraft Lodges had changed their *purposes, mission statements, and business plans.* No longer were these Lodges concerned with bringing in new members who were strictly interested in making a living by plying the trade of Stonecraft. No longer were they pursuing Patrons to pay for their Stonecraft products and services. No longer were they focusing upon plying their Stonecraft trade and training their members to do the same. From all outward signs, they closed the door to the Stonecraft trade and opened another to a whole different line of work that changed what they did forever and they did so with unbelievably creative zeal!

There are two typical references cited for the introduction of non-Stonecraft members being permitted to join what is now known as Operative Craft Lodges. The first recorded information related to members joining these Stonecraft Lodges who didn't join to learn the Trade were Sir Robert Moray and Elias Ashmole.

According to one Stonecraft Lodge's records, R. Moray was admitted into its Lodge in May 1641 CE. E. Ashmole joined another Stonecraft Lodge a few years later, according to a diary entry attributed to him and written in July 1646 CE. Neither man joined to learn the Stonecraft profession.

Many other men also joined Stonecraft Lodges over the next fifty or so years who clearly did not join them to learn the trade of Stonecraft. It was also clear that each new member was offered membership into Stonecraft Lodges, each went through some form of ceremony based upon Stonecraft Charges and Obligations to become members and each was not interested in joining to learn Stonecraft.

By about 1717 CE, four Lodges in London came together at a local ale-house[e] to create a governing Organization that would come to be known as a Grand Lodge. The purpose of this organization was not to perpetuate or preserve Stonecraft in any way. We are led to believe that its purpose was to standardize and regulate the practice of Ritual Performances, which until that time had gone wholly unregulated. Ritual at that time was largely non-uniform in the many Lodges that had begun to allow non-trade members.

With two Ritual Performances called *The Entered Apprentice and Fellow Craft Degrees,* the Grand Lodge had established itself as the governing body which all associated Lodges must respect and follow.

---

[e] The Goose & Gridiron Ale-house

Within a very short amount of years (~1721 CE), the restrictions the new Grand Lodge placed upon its undertaking prevented easy replication. Membership grew to the point where new Lodges needed to be constituted.

New Lodges could be formed at that time but the restrictions required the Master of the Lodge to be of Fellow Craft rank. The problem faced by the new venture was that the Fellow Craft Degree could only be performed by the Grand Lodge itself. To extricate itself from this responsibility and to allow replication of Lodges to occur without the Grand Lodge being required to perform the necessary Degree work, a solution was provided.

According to several sources, the Entered Apprentice Degree of the time was split up, thereby creating two Degrees. The first portion continued to be referred to as *The Entered Apprentice Degree* while the second portion created by this division was named thereafter *The Fellow Craft Degree.* [35, 36, 37] This division of the Apprentice Degree into two Degrees allowed Lodges to perform both sections. This split also allowed them to make both Entered Apprentices and the required Fellow Crafts necessary to supply future Lodge Masters.

Meanwhile, the initial second Degree which was known as *The Master's Part* still remained in practice but was done so rarely. It was originally honorably conferred upon the person who held the building contract on the site.[38] It was also the first *"High Degree"* in that it was not truly part of what was initially required to join the Society and become a full member. It was added only after the Society had fully formed.

Interestingly enough, *The Master's Part,* now known as the Master Degree was not initially widely performed. It did not become a requirement for full membership in the Society till many years later.

Funding

The funding for Stonecraft Lodges up until this shift in focus came from Patrons who wanted the expertise and products of the Society's members. That changed very quickly once it became clear that Patrons who wanted to experience these performances would gladly pay for both:

a) *The right to do so as the main focus of the performance and*
b) *The right to participate thereafter as either an important supporting cast member or merely to watch the performance from the sidelines and to participate as needed by any one specific performance.*

This shift in product and service by these Lodges produced both initial upfront funding from those who wanted to go through the available Degrees at the time and from those who wanted to participate in Lodge activities thereafter. The initial upfront fees (Degree fees) and the reoccurring residual membership fees (Annual dues) provided all the necessary funding for each Lodge's expenses, if the fees were correctly assessed and properly managed. Additional funding occurred occasionally and came from benefactors in the form of donations; much as it occurs to this day.

Competition

Many Brothers who have taken the time to explore the history of Freemasonry are well aware that there existed a schism between the Premier Grand Lodge and another Grand Lodge that formed in 1751 CE. It was called the *"Most Ancient and Honourable Society of Free and Accepted Masons according to the Old Constitutions",* but it is now commonly referred to as *"The Grand Lodge of the Antients"*. It was started by six unaffiliated Lodges with primarily Irish membership.

With the intensity of a tsunami, the leaders of this younger Grand Lodge attacked the Premier Grand Lodge and soon thereafter, the younger of the two had a sizable backing of Lodges and members who performed its own Freemasonic plays. These plays were similar but they had enough noticeable differences to make it distinct from the other Grand Lodge's plays.

There were many issues that each Grand Lodge had with each other's renderings but eventually, the two found enough common ground to reconcile their differences. Once certain compromises occurred, the two eventually merged in 1813 CE and formed what is now known as *"The United Grand Lodge of England"*. Due to propagation of their separate and distinct plays over the years of their rivalry and even during their reconciliation years, Freemasonic Organizations have a wide diversity of Rituals spread around the globe.

EMBLEMATIC STRUCTURE OF FREEMASONRY

Explosion

The desire to participate in more of these types of plays was evident by the eagerness of the membership to participate. The turnkey operation and related franchise formula the Premier Grand

Lodge had created was a hit. Membership continued to increase and the Organization as a whole expanded quickly.

It was shortly after the formation of the Premier Grand Lodge, its first Degree split and the inclusion of the Master's Part as the first High Degree that further innovations occurred. The demand for more Freemasonic plays increased. Based on market needs, more Freemasonic plays were scripted and offered to the membership for additional fees and dues. Men did not hesitate to step up to pay for the Rites and the right to see them again and again thereafter.

Each additional Degree came with its own fabricated history. Each script was based enough upon existing histories and lore and laced with enticing allusion to have enough validity to immerse the patrons into an imaginative and artificial reality. These realities were all steeped with connections to the original Stonecraft and creative connections to other histories. Each had rich moral and religious overtones and had enough twists and allusions as to allow additional connections that would set the stage for the Degrees that were to follow.

Eventually two entirely different Degree directions emerged and where accepted as authentic, at least within the lore created by the Society, to eventually form the current York and Scottish Rite Degrees.

The York Rite was extensively experiential. It was deeply religious based and it put forth a claim that it both completed the first three Degrees and provided what was lost within the context of the Blue Lodge Drama. They are meant to be experienced by the Candidates fully.

The Scottish Rite was expansively philosophical and lesson laced. Although exemplified in total and sometimes in part, its complete set of Degrees is often performed in some Jurisdictions over several two weekend increments usually separated by six months. The intensity of these weekend events has been likened to trying to drink water from a fully discharging fire hose. Even Candidates superior in the art of learning and who are used to taking in large volumes of information are often quickly overwhelmed by the manner to which these Degrees are currently offered.

The two directions form the basis for what are now known as the High Degrees and have their own governing bodies associated with their operations and memberships.

Franchise Success

With the initial creation of the first Franchising body, Freemasonic plays had become available to anyone who met the base requirements for joining. Lodge creation occurred worldwide within countries that allowed them and the Freemasonic system of Total Immersion Plays soon came to be recognized as sought after experiences by many.

While all this was occurring, the membership soon forgot that the entire system was primarily self-supported theater that protected itself by highly regulating those who could join and those who have joined. Members became so entrenched in the subject matter upon which the theatrical productions focused that they soon all lost sight of what they were actually doing.

This condition continues to this day and there is likely to be little change until Grand Lodges educate their members and the public as to what the Craft actually is and what it does.

Regularity

From Freemasonry's beginning, any Lodge who called itself *Regular* had to conform to specific standards prescribed by its Grand Lodge. Part of these standards involved being granted permission to create a Lodge. Charters were expected to be obtained through an established Grand Lodge. In this respect, Organizations that claim to be legitimately Freemasonic are Franchises. Charters are akin to Licenses that are issued by the Franchising body and without such a written document, no Work is considered legitimate, even if it is performed exactly how a Chartered Lodge would perform the very same work.

Competitive Echoes

There are other consequences for forgetting the Craft's roots and for not educating the membership and the public about Society origins and what the Society actually does. Although there were two Grand Lodges who had reconciled their differences in 1813, there now exist hundreds of Grand Lodges that go unrecognized around the globe due to discrepancies in how they came to be. As much as the Premier Grand Lodge made earnest effort to keep what they did privately owned, they and others who have come together over the years in unity have never been successful in preventing newly created Grand Lodges from using their privately owned materials.   And there are new ones coming into being annually.

Although education is a key to minimizing such activities, the manner which Freemasonry keeps their materials private has worked against them. The public is as ill-informed about Freemasonry's Performances as is its general membership. As a result, potential members do not realize when they are being courted by or when they are joining an illegitimate organization.[39]

VIII. The Freemasonic Ceremonies

*The Phrase "A Peculiar System of Morality" is
perhaps the most misunderstood Description of
Freemasonry that anyone within or without the
Craft shall ever encounter, till now.*

When you didn't know the original meanings behind
the words *Peculiar* and *Morality* you might think them to
mean *odd* and *righteousness* respectively. Accepting these
as their meanings, you would not come close to the true
meaning trying to be conveyed by those who understood
these words at the time of their initial offering.

Since Freemasonry's beginnings, it is clear that their
plays have been successful in keeping people interested,
both inside and outside the Organization. They are written
with specific attributes that have universal appeal to those
who engage in them and those who desire to find hidden

truths within them. These attributes pique the interest of individuals who seek to uncover the mysteries of life and to participate in activities that exemplify that searching spirit.

When you evaluate these plays, you find that all of them have the same attributes in common.

1) **Time Immemorial** – Claim Ancient Origins and Presuppose Pre-existence.
2) **Common Threads** – Base it upon Universally Accepted Morality, especially one that is already familiar to Candidates.
3) **Cloak in Mystery** – Hint at everything, but never be definitive unless it is an accepted belief.
4) **Tease** – Give just enough information to keep interest high with hints that there's much more.
5) **Amplify & Connect** – Make things appear bigger than they actually are.
6) **Make it Unfamiliar** – Use archaic language that has modern day meanings that redirect those who do not look into archaic or obsolete meanings.
7) **Make it Familiar** – Associate it with a multitude of well-established things, events, beliefs and people who are known.
8) **Allude** – Use Allegory, Metaphor and literary references throughout.
9) **Privatize** – Keep it *Peculiar*.
10) **Restrict Access** – Limit viewers (by Membership only).
11) **Initiation** – Have it be more than a play; obligate the participants to engage in and to live the play's themes into the future.
12) **Standardization** – Assure that the script dictating Ritual and those who may experience it never change.
13) **Culture** – Develop, Cultivate and Support a culture that lives what it portrays.

Let's take a look at each element that makes up the Morality that constitutes each Degree and supporting Rituals.

Time Immemorial

"Time Immemorial" is a phrase that has a distinct meaning. It means *time extending beyond the reach of memory, record, or tradition.* It also implies *indefinitely ancient,* as in *"ancient beyond memory or record".*[40] It also has an impact upon those who hear it. By assuming its meaning, hearing the claim of Time Immemorial establishes within the minds of naive listeners that what they are experiencing has occurred for others since before memories of it could be recalled. The impression it leaves is that their experience has also been experienced by others from before the dawn of mankind's memory.

This is a very impressive message to those who experience it. When it is affective, it will draw Candidates from the current reality of their life and into one that is now reframed with history. They are invited to think beyond their present and connect themselves with a substantially rich past with others who have done what they are doing in the moment.

It should be of some interest too that this English based term where the adjective is a postmodifier is influenced by Norman French; especially since the phrase was most likely incorporated into the English Mystery plays (Miracle and Morality) that migrated from France.

Legally, the term *Time Immemorial* has come to mean that a property owner has enjoyed the benefits of use for such a long time that proof of ownership is no longer required. It is simply accepted and cannot be contested.

More formally, the term has been defined by English Law and its derivatives as "time out of mind,[41]" and "a time before legal history and beyond legal memory.[42]" The first Statute of Westminster put forth in 1275 CE that *Time Immemorial* was limited to the reign of Richard I (Richard the Lionheart), beginning 6 July 1189 CE, which was the date of the King's accession.[43] From then on, use of any right or proof of unbroken possession made it unnecessary to establish the original grant under certain circumstances.

Time Immemorial was re-defined in 1832 CE. It was then accepted as *"Time whereof the Memory of Man runneth not to the contrary"*.[44] Onward from that point in time, dating legal memory from a fixed time was abandoned. Replacing it was the understanding that rights which had been enjoyed for twenty years (or as against the Crown at least thirty years) should not be impeached merely by proving that they had not been enjoyed before (holding by adverse possession).[45]

Interestingly enough, the *High Court of Chivalry* is said to have defined the period before 1066 CE as *Time Immemorial* for the purposes of heraldry.[46] The year 1066 should be noted as important to Freemasonry in general since it is the demarcation date that separates Old English and Modern English. After the Norman Conquest of 1066, the fairly rich inflection system of Old English broke down and the beginnings of Modern English seeded itself over the next 100 years. Along with this was the addition of foreign words which were incorporated into the native vocabulary unaltered from their original use.[47]

As an aside, this influence of French can be seen in the use of Synonymia[f] within Ritual. Furthermore, "…in the twelfth and thirteenth centuries language in England was

---

[f] In rhetoric, Synonymia (Greek: syn, "alike" + onoma, "name") is the use of several synonyms together to amplify or explain a given subject, term or idea. Within Ritual, it is a purposeful repetition intended to add emotional force and intellectual clarity.

part Norman-French and part Anglo-Saxon and that early Stonecraft writers, desiring to make sure that no misunderstanding was possible, often expressed ideas in word pairs, one word from each language. Hence such phrases as *'hele and conceal', 'parts and points',* and *'free will and accord'"* [48] are sprinkled throughout Ritual.

Taking all this into consideration, and adding to this the fact the vernacular plays (~900 CE) from which Freemasonic Ritual take their origin, it can be easily seen that the *Time Immemorial* referenced within Freemasonic Ritual is denoting those times prior to 1066 CE.

Common Threads

All faiths have within them common moral threads that are universally accepted, especially by those who seek to experience and support them. Sown into Freemasonic productions are Moral themes that are easily accepted and willingly embraced by those members who want them most in their lives.

The appeal of these common threads makes Ritual a very enjoyable and affirming experience to participate in, to view or to read. Unless distorted by hidden agendas, these common threads speak warmly to the hearts of those who encounter them. This occurs even more so when the Morality spoken of is one that the Candidates have sought for some time with marginal success.

Shroud it in Mystery

Both the Freemasonic Organization and its Rituals have been shrouded in mystery from its beginnings. Each has very little overt information put forth that clearly states, "here are our beginnings".

As a result, what has occurred is varied and creative research by serious truth seekers of every form and fancy. They have taken it upon themselves to navigate the twisted paths that they earnestly believe are set down by Freemasonry. There are hoards of amateur and professional sleuths that have approached the subject. Each has been called by the mystery sirens to investigate for himself a puzzle that has many doors and keys and no true final stage. Once the investigation starts, and a possible solution is discovered, it only brings forth a legion of other questions.

It truly is a never ending task should you desire to do this yourself and it has kept Masonic researchers busy for lifetimes of intrigue.

Of course, intriguing plays also have many entangled elements of Mystery. To create this affect masterfully, specific techniques are employed though the use of veils or cloaking devices. For maximum impact, all senses are usually employed to immerse the recipients sensually into what is offered. But for Organizational purposes, only Visual, Tangible and Auditory components are employed.

They might be employed through the use of out of sight contributions that are not seen by the central focus of the play's attention. They include allusions to things that are not immediately obvious to those who do not consciously recognize the allusions at first. They might also be physical barriers such as curtains or the use of hoodwinks at times to heighten the participants attention to what is being offered to other senses. There are many with deeper meanings and associations connected with the references employed.

It also helps to continually state and imply at certain strategic points in the Performance that all that is being revealed is secret and only known to a few worthy individuals. This is a technique used in storytelling to elicit the understanding that what is being provided is not shared with just anyone. It also communicates that the audience participants are special.

Teasers

Freemasonic Ritual is pocked full of teasing elements. Anyone who has experienced or even read through them knows this is true. What's more, Progression through each play provides just enough information to satisfy some aspect of a curiosity. It also provides to those who want more additional elements that indicate bluntly that there is so much more. It consistently conveys that these other satisfying elements shall not be delivered currently.

One of the greatest Freemasonic teases is that of The Master's Word. It is itself ineffable, which makes it impossible to communicate through written or oral effort. Members are told that it existed at one time, but was lost due to an unfortunate event. There are awkward efforts to share what The Word is in plays that follow the one where it is first mentioned. Unfortunately, even when it is supposedly shared, how it is shared violates what is known about it. This only leaves those members wanting closure on what they seek further teased.

Amplify

Freemasonry has incorporated the ability to amplify its attributes through allusion to things that it claims are part of its history. It does this masterfully and continually; and at times to its detriment, by overzealous authors making effort to make it more than it actually is. Such enthusiastic writers have taken Ritual's basic lead and endeavored to expand upon it in every possible direction and in every possible way.

This trend has continued to exist from its very beginning. As things stand, there is a high probability that this trend shall continue far into the future until the Craft itself goes through an insightful conversion that inoculates future generations against such nonsense. As it is now, the mass of Brothers has yet to develop any stable immunity against it. Most encourage it and hence are carriers of this disease.

Unfamiliar

Freemasonry is ripe with archaic and obsolete words and phrases. Unless you are familiar with them through other means, you are likely to be overwhelmed with their abundance. It is disorienting to some and enchanting to others. This mix of reactions allows for Ritual to keep the interest of even those who have been exposed to it many times over.

This archaic and obsolete addition to Freemasonry's scripts brings forth certain airs of mysticism and esoteric feels that are akin to many religious, philosophical and spiritually based writings and practice. Anyone who is exposed to Freemasonic Ritual, either through participation or through discussion, shall quickly gather that both the words and the method to which the words are used are not common to everyday manners.

Familiar

Freemasonic Ritual and Lectures touch upon a myriad of themes, phrases, beliefs, concepts and historical figures. This addition to its scripts has provided to its Candidates many familiar touch stones that help keep them comfortable while they are experiencing something altogether different. Such Landmarks make navigating unfamiliar territories easier as new features of the landscape are added to the old.

Allusions

Throughout Freemasonic Ritual are carefully placed allusions. These allusions use masterfully constructed allegories and metaphors that have many levels of meaning, depending upon the experience of the person going through them. Compounding these are many sprinkled references to known historical and literary figures, situations, times and places that, if an individual is well read, shall bring to mind a flood of connections to what is being put forth in the moment.

Coupled with all these elements are liberally spread instructions explaining some of these allusions in a different light. They are masterfully interlaced also for they are designed to introduce new thoughts to those experiencing them. Their interlacing is also just enough to let the individuals experiencing them to know that, should someone explore them further, they shall find more connections and reap the benefits of their efforts.

For individuals who like exploring, such information is experienced as a treasure map of potential fun. They also find that the exploration is endless. Should they enjoy such activities, they experience delight with every new discovery and new mystery to explore.

Privatize

Perhaps the most misunderstood aspect of Freemasonic Rituals is why they are not written down for the general membership in many Jurisdictions. Most want to believe that this is because members don't want to have any of their secrets revealed outside the Organization. This is truly the driving factor that many hold as the real reason behind keeping Ritual private, but it is not the underlying reason.

Freemasonic plays, to have their full affect, must not be read before they are experienced firsthand. To read or discuss the play prior to its occurrence ruins the experience for the Candidate. This is why Freemasonic Organizations have made every effort to keep them *Peculiar* in the original not modern sense of the word. This makes more sense when you realize that the word *Peculiar* originally meant *"Privately Owned"*.

The effort to keep Freemasonic plays out of the Candidate's hands prior to them experiencing it has not been without its troubles. There have been numerous individuals who, after experiencing these plays for themselves, have taken this privately owned materials and had it printed for retail distribution to the general public.

Unfortunately, countless Candidates have their experience of these plays tainted. They never had the chance to experience them fresh and as they were meant to be experienced. Some greedily published the Degree materials and others thoughtlessly shared this information with Candidates prior to their Lodge experience.

Restrict Access

To experience a Freemasonic play, you must volunteer to do so of your free will and accord. You might be told that you would make a good Mason, but the general rules of most all Jurisdictions are that blatant solicitation is not allowed.

Coupled with this requirement are others that assure that long term membership potentials are maximized.

You must be between nonage and dotage to join. Nonage might be anywhere below age eighteen or twenty-five years of age, depending upon the Jurisdiction and family involvement. In the other direction, Dotage is a man who is considered senile. No man who shows signs of senility shall be considered.

These restrictions increase the possibility that no one immature or senile, and therefore undesirable, shall experience the play. It is believed that the plays require a certain maturity and mentality to appreciate fully. These requirements have an added bonus to the society in that they lend themselves to a certain age range of men who are potentially mature and capable long-term members.

It is also understood that a man must be of good rapport and come highly recommended. This covers two distinct aspects of membership. Being of good rapport speaks to a man's reputation. By prequalifying Candidates to assure that they have good reputations, they are likely to be members of the same ilk. Secondly, if a man comes well-recommended, he is more probably surrounded by men who are likely Candidates themselves.

In addition to all these requirements, there is a religious requirement. For Lodges Recognized by the United Grand Lodges of England (UGLE), Scotland and Ireland, belief in God or a Supreme Being is required. Every member who Petitions is required to state this belief if they are to be seriously considered for membership. Freemasonic Ritual is filled with references to God, including prayers that call upon God in the role of The Grand Architect of the Universe, all playing upon Masonic themes. All their plays would come across absolutely foolish, meaningless or useless to someone who didn't believe in what was being portrayed. These plays have a specific target audience to which they must be directed to have their desired impact.

All these requirements lend themselves to good members who support the entire arena of portrayals and good future members who potentially shall do the same.

Initiate

One of the most compelling themes played out by Freemasonic plays is that of Initiation. One does not merely experience the plays, one is asked to take them seriously and to engage in them totally. This engagement is to the point that one should feel obligated to what the play portrays. In fact, parts of the plays involve Obligations that are administered and considered to be solemnly binding to those embracing the play. This means that all the concepts, thoughts, allusions, Obligations and Charges are to be taken to be an embraced reality. Those who experience these plays are expected to fulfill them over the remainder of their lifetime.

It is intent of the Society that the themes portrayed by these plays should continue to engage participants long after it is experienced. Even if it may take a lifetime, the participants are expected to make every effort to follow through to the best of their abilities and within their own personal, professional and religious limitations.

And such engagement is not expected to be solely within their time participating in Lodge activities. Communicated throughout all the plays and through its players are the expectations that Candidates are to live the script inside and outside the Lodge and do so without wavering. Furthermore, the reach of the Society extends far beyond the Lodge in that failure to live this script in all aspects of their lives might and shall jeopardize their membership in the Society.

The message that the Society communicates through all this is that you should not join on a whim. You must plan to adhere to its premises and principles.

As an aside, Initiation is a primary goal of the Freemasonic Society. It is not well known by modern day Freemasons, but it was so well known in its beginning that the very title of the Organization speaks to this goal.

Part of the Official Organizational title adopted in its early history was *"Free & Accepted Masons"*. Members have since early on referred to themselves as *Freemasons,* alluding to the Free Masons for whom they fashioned their plays around. Although they refer to themselves in this way, in reality they are *Accepted* Masons only, for the word *Free* at that time meant *"Superior"* and *"Excellent"* and it indicated a Stonecraft Mason whose skills enabled him to practice his trade as a Master Craftsman or Journeyman. Those labeled *"Accepted"* were just that, Initiated members of the Society only. At that time, the word *Accepted* meant a person who had *Entered; Joined; been Made; been Initiated in* the Society.[49]

Since that time, men have been referring to themselves as Freemasons not knowing that they were simply saying that they had joined the Society and pay dues to continue to claim that association as dues paying members.

Standardize

One of the key components laid down by the Grand Lodge effort was to assure that both the plays and the requirement as to those who may experience them should never change. This is in essence the creation of a turn-key system that, if followed, guaranteed specific results. In effect, by creating a Grand Lodge system with supporting standards, it created a Franchise which facilitated the wholesale replication of its System of *Morality* (as in *"morality plays"*) that was indeed *Peculiar* (privately owned) by it and it alone.

This Ritual and audience standardization from its beginning allowed for some quality control over what was being put forth to its target audience. It also assured that the target audience itself was proper and receptive to its purposes.

By around 1723 CE, these standards became both promulgated to all Recognized (associated) Lodges and their members and canonized along the Organization's intentions of the time. Belief in God became a requirement for acceptance. Females, which until this point in time were permitted into the Stonecraft society albeit in very low numbers, were then proscribed from even being considered for membership in what was next offered. Members Obligated themselves along specific lines that require rectitude of conduct that would cause harsh Societal ramifications if not adhered to (Reprimand, Suspension or Expulsion).

In effect, the actual Foundation of the Freemasonic Society was laid in those moments. It moved away from being *a way for Lodges to add revenue to their coffers by allowing benefactors as Patrons to experience two initiations and continue to pay dues to view the same into the future. It moved toward being a Theatrical Franchise cloaked by a façade of Stonecraft traditions and initiation rites that are not practiced by any of its members beyond their consistent portrayal and conveyance to its newest members.* Independent Lodges that put on their own versions of these plays slowly became known by the Recognized Lodges as irregular and clandestine. As a result, they remained unrecognized and hence not part of the Society.

Culture

Freemasonry as an Organization has created a culture around its plays. Its Ceremonial plays are called *Rituals* and *Degrees* and no one within the Organization usually refers to them differently. Most members within the Organization would consider it disturbingly disrespectful for anyone to even begin to imply that the Rituals and Degrees it practices and performs ceremonially were plays of any sort.

This stands in the face of what many within the Society experience outside the Blue Lodge arena. Many of the non-Blue Lodge Degrees are replete with theatrical materials used to train and guide those who perform these plays called *Higher Degrees.* These theatric references, materials and overt training are surprisingly absent at the Blue Lodge level. This is unfortunate too as it would most likely be a welcome relief to the multitudes who have come through them and found the dogmatic illusions, thoughtless role playing and never dropped in-characterizations disturbing enough to leave when discovered.

The Blue Lodge culture never discusses the actual Craft in which they engage. They use the Craft throughout their formal and informal engagements with others, never lifting the mask off of what they are actually doing – *Theater.*

IX.   The Craft Purpose

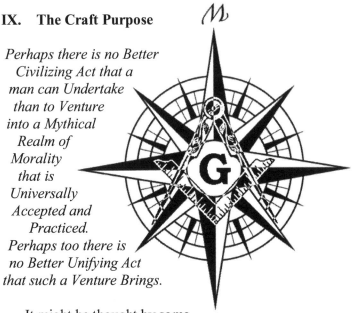

*Perhaps there is no Better
    Civilizing Act that a
 man can Undertake
    than to Venture
 into a Mythical
    Realm of
 Morality
    that is
 Universally
 Accepted and
    Practiced.
Perhaps too there is
 no Better Unifying Act
that such a Venture Brings.*

It might be thought by some men to be something that is simply common sense to talk about the reasons behind teaching Morality. It might be something that many people take for granted as just a really good idea. Yet the reasons for teaching Morality go far beyond good manners and civil decency. Morality is the Foundation of greatness for both the individual and a society made up of those individuals. When you want to Build a Society that lasts, you must first Establish a Strong Foundation of Morality. Anything less shall doom it to oblivion.

From its beginning, the Foundation that supports all Freemasonic Societies is first and foremost one of Morality. It is the one true underpinning that shores it up

without fail; *and fails when it is not used to shore it up.*
Without it the Trust that men would normally place in one
another is unlikely to occur. Without it agreements
between men would be continually in question. Without it
relationships would be filled with overwhelming doubt.
The presence of Morality is the underlying fabric that holds
the whole of Society together.

The Order

The Society of Freemasons was built upon the
Foundation of Morality. Its Codes, Performances and
Rules all echo this one fact and does so overwhelmingly.
In this respect, without Morality, the entire nature of
Freemasonic Society, as most know of it and experience it
today, would not exist.

The reality of Morality is that it *brings order to chaos.*
It lessens specific uncertainties in relationships and enables
men to focus on things that might normally be hindered
without it. In this respect, Morality brings investment in
activities that would go wholly unsupported had it not been
present from the start. No other reality binds men together
better and for good purpose than the strong cord of a Moral
Obligation.

The Society's focus is upon a privately owned system
that is intended to provide Performances that are supposed
to convey moral teachings. The Performances are
allegorical in nature and are laced with references to
Scripture and Philosophy, among many other things. Each
Performance has many sections and each section is rich
with Symbols that are verbal, visual and physical.

From all outward appearances, the Performances
provide an abundance of Moral guidance to those who
experience them, no matter how one might participate.

The Reality

Unfortunately, the Society itself doesn't focus upon Moral training, at least, not directly or with deliberate and consistent purpose. Even though it makes effort to teach Morality through its allegorical plays, it is too often misunderstood or missed altogether. Many who experience these Performances are so uninformed about the literary and historical references it uses or its symbols and signs that the significance of the lessons is missed almost entirely. As a result, members may go through several Degrees never understanding what they are offered by these allegorical plays.

In reality, good Performances of well-written plays don't have to be explained afterward. They speak directly to the heart and soul of those who experience them. They use well-chosen metaphors, allegorical references and suitable symbols that are familiar to all those who experience them. The significance is grasped immediately by the audience, even if that audience is part of the Performance. As a result, it transforms.

The Road to Perdition

Realizing this, there have been some Jurisdictions that have modernized their plays in the hope that they will be better understood and better embraced by the new cast members. Unfortunately, modernizing plays in this way often cheapens them. This is because one of the purposes of these plays it to introduce men to archaic language in preparation for further study of the ancient roots of their own chosen Faiths.

There are very few men who do not have to learn an ancient language to better understand the original words used within their Faith. Most well-established religions have ritual that is saturated with archaic words, phrases, signs and symbols. Some have made effort to modernize them and have them spoken in the native tongue of the people who practice it. Others have traditions that rule out such innovations. These religions lean more toward educating the members of their Faith on the meanings,

significances and applications of these ancient rituals toward modern day life.

Freemasonic Society would benefit from such examples. There are Faiths that require specific study of its ritual language, culture, laws, traditions, symbols, histories, heritages and other Faith related topics before one may be allowed to practice it. This is not to say that Freemasonry is a Faith in any way. It is to say that far too many Jurisdictions leave vital education solely to the individual. They might provide officer training and tests that offer a precursory education as to the laws of the organization, but extremely few actually offer in depth education and cultivation of the very morality that is espoused by the Ritual the Organization painstakingly preserves. If you were to observe what educational support is actually provided, you would quickly see that preservation of Ritual and the Organization are overwhelmingly preferred and practiced over the actual application of the Principles they preserve.

How does the Organization change this? It has to first get honest about what it truly does provide. Currently, that is theater. If that theater is to have anything substantial supporting the Morality it is supposed to be conveying, then the Society must support education that helps make good men Better.

A Quick Review

Freemasonry is a *Theatrical Society.* The Craft it practices is *acting.* The Scripts it follows were originally based upon the ancient initiation rites of the Stoneworker's guilds and that is the Mask that it wears night and day. The Organization was fabricated to convey Morality in the hopes that it would provide improvement incentives to all those who join. Its products are plays, opportunity to commit to Betterment and memberships. Much has been added to its endeavors over the years that continually emphasize further commitment to living a Moral life.

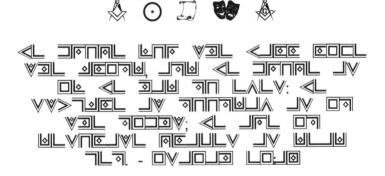

X. The Allusions to Truth

*No matter how you choose to Believe,
your Belief shall engage you regardless.*

Joseph Campbell had some keen observations about people who engage in religious activities. He stated that there were basically two types of individuals who participate. The first one does not know that they are engaging in a metaphor, they truly believe the metaphors explain reality and they willingly engage in it because of this chosen belief. The second type knows that the religion they practice is only a metaphorical attempt to capture what cannot be truly captured; they know this and they willingly engage in the metaphor anyway.

He further stated that they both obtain immeasurable value out of their engagement, but they have totally different views as to what they practice.

There exist these two types within the Freemasonic Society too. The former joins it, usually embraces it in the same fashion as he does his Faith and accepts what is offered as a confirmation of what he believes of his Faith. The later joins and finds a playground brimming with activities and materials whose potential shimmers with further engagement. He keeps in mind that it's there for his further enlightenment, but never does he mislead himself to believe it to be anything other than a playground.

The interesting thing to note here is that both types find reward and fulfillment in their Societal participation. Both engage for reasons of their own choosing and which are right for them. Each sits and stands side by side with the other in complete enjoyment of what they receive.

And what makes this harmony possible is partially due to the allusions that the Society has Masterfully chosen to bring both together.

Ritual

There is no doubt that Freemasonic Degree Ritual is dripping with allusions toward literature, mythology, religion and philosophy. Its richness is overwhelming to the literate and irresistible to those eager to learn more. Included within it are references to great works. Shakespeare, Plato, Plutarch and others are all scribed neatly into its scripts. Religious Scripture, Philosophy and Theology are also all intertwined within its pseudo-ancient archives. Symbols used within Cabala, Hermeticism, Alchemy, Metallurgy, Religion and Politics are also sprinkled within it as trail markers for the literate and as breadcrumbs left for hungry birds. There is little that escapes its wide offering and few eager men are not drawn to its subtle play.

There are many who are driven by curiosity; to discover all that they can, hoping to find yet one more idea that can be connected with things that are already known. Freemasonic plays have driven many a man, who would have otherwise sat idle, to contemplate mysteries he would have dismissed had they been presented in different settings.

Yet, by its very nature, the Craft plays have engaged these men and have done so in Grand fashion.

The Society plays answer the ancient question, *"How do you bring together men of different races, different ages, different cultures, different faiths and different capacities?"* It does so with astounding success.

Mystery to the Craft

It's been only a little over a decade that I have been a member of the Society of Free & Accepted Masons. When I first Entered the Organization and was permitted through the West Gate, I was exposed to these Degree Performances. Characters that I knew well greeted me through the Ritual that was provided to me by Lodge members. I was embraced by many references to stories from my youth. The Rituals felt comfortable. They felt familiar. It felt like I was at home.

This experience was not the same though for other men who had passed through that same West Gate for the first time. I soon found out that many of the Candidates coming through were not familiar with the Classics. They had not read the writings of Plato, Socrates, Plutarch, or Homer. They had not read through any Holy Scriptures much less knew to what The Book of Ruth, Psalms, Kings, Chronicles, Ecclesiastes, or Ezra refer. They were not illiterate. They were merely uninformed due to a lack of exposure.

I found too that a few of the Candidates knew the references. They had not however taken the time in their years to delve deeply into any of them or to perpend even superficially the significant messages that is offered to each generation. They all Entered into the Society's Performances like blind men to a portrait studio, never truly experiencing as was intended the brilliant Works on display for their enjoyment.

Meaningless Initiation

This saddened me immensely. The entirety of Degree Performances is staged Initiation Rites. I know from experience and from much research that Initiation Rites are intended to transform the consciousness of those who go through them. To accomplish this, those experiencing them must comprehend the significance of what they are presented. To experience them and not comprehend the significance of what is before them leaves Candidates empty and puzzled. Not knowing what the references and symbols mean, they are more likely to ask, *"Is that all there is?"* afterward, rather than exclaim in jubilation, *"Wow! What a Ride!"*

To Enlighten or not to Enlighten, that is the Challenge!

I have heard all too often from well-meaning Brothers that you don't want to ever share anything with pre-masons that would spoil the mystery. I agree! It is important not to share *what* is to be experienced.

But their attitude is also one that supports the notion that to naively go through something that is mysterious is much more important that to experience something for the first time that has significant and substantial meaning toward one's life. Their attitude and view leaves me perpetually puzzled for it seems to me that the later would have much more of a positive impact upon initiates than the former. After all, who wants to go to a subtitled foreign film blind folded?

Wouldn't it make sense to teach men the significance of Ritual in general? What is it supposed to activate within them? What is the significance of certain symbols, words and gestures to a man, to what they refer within specific moments in history and how they have been viewed in the past? The amount of additional materials that have been added to Freemasonic plays over the years boggles the mind. Did it never occur to script writers that overwhelmed minds can't grasp what these plays offer? Wouldn't proper preparation include educating the man, not in what he shall experience, but in the significance of the words, phrases, gestures, symbols and allusions that he shall encounter on his journey?

So many men go through these plays, never having any understanding as to who the characters are, what the symbols mean and how the plays have any relevance to them.

There are members that exist today who claim that this way of sharing Light should be enough to keep men interested sufficient to stick around with equally uninformed men who guess at what it all means. I believe that they are mistaken in these beliefs.

Without a foundation in classical literature, scripture and related materials, there is little likelihood of any man truly appreciating anything other the superficial aspects of what the Society offers him. What's more, when they don't appreciate what is offered, they do not stick around much longer than is absolutely necessary.

Penetralia

This lack of Foundation is perhaps why so many members believe pre-masons should remain uninformed before they experience the Freemasonic plays. When you truly study Ritual, you soon discover the Degrees convey no secrets. Everything that Rituals convey points you toward something that you must find elsewhere, if you are not already aware of these things.

This Light that is found elsewhere is not referring to exposures about Freemasonry. They actually reveal no secrets either. Freemasonic Ritual and Lectures point you toward knowledge that has to be obtained elsewhere because you shall not in any way or form receive it through Freemasonic activities sponsored by any one particular Grand Lodge. The few words, grips and signs sprinkled about that are called *secrets* are nothing more than *Modes of Recognition* anyone can obtain. Yet, should they be used by non-members, they would soon be discovered to be a fraud. There is so much more to these Modes than merely knowing what they are.

Granted, there are some things that as a member you are asked not to share. This is not because they are secret, but because by keeping things to yourself, you primarily do not ruin it for those who have yet to experience these theatrical productions. Secondarily to this, by keeping things to yourself you develop a much needed discipline in your life that shall change you and it for the Better. They are not secret. They are merely not discussed with those who have yet to legitimately go through the ceremonial plays that the Society offers to qualified Candidates.

XI. Membership Screening

The only way to Improve the Odds of a Successful Grand and Important Undertaking is to Assure all those who might Participate are already pre-qualified to Take the Journey. Anything less would Sabotage the Trip.

The Freemasonic Society from its start had to assure that it would last. To improve its survival odds, it made sure that anyone interested in joining would have the right qualities to support what it was making effort to do. Men of specific character were allowed to Enter, and should they continue to show favorable character, they would progress toward other membership benefits. The intent was to Accept only the right Candidates. These same intentions exist today, although some members could use a few well-placed reminders.

The Society's Goal

The challenge for the Organization from its very beginning was clear: *To Bring Order to Chaos.* To do so a vehicle was chosen to deliver it. That Vehicle was *"The*

Craft". But before you assume that the Craft is what you believe it to be, let's describe the Craft that is Practiced by Society Members.

1) Proactive Volunteerism
2) Qualifying
3) Progression
4) Harmony
5) Status Quo
6) Purposefulness

Let's review them one by one.

Proactive Volunteerism

Potential Members must be Proactive in regard to wanting to join the ranks of the membership. They must continue this afterward should they wish to participate in Lodge activities.

Should they fail to proactively volunteer, subtle prompting shall be employed by other members to act as a catalyst and to train the member to do this on his own. This training starts from the very beginning by his voluntarily joining the Society and continues if the member's interests can be kept. Training is thought to be effective when members don't say *no* to work requests or simply do work that needs to be done without having been asked.

Qualifying

Potential Members are screened for specific Qualities and are Accepted along these lines. Age range, belief systems, reputation and, above all, Morality are all aspects that are scrutinized. As prescribed by the Society, Candidates are to be rejected if anything in their character and background appeared to be unsupportive of it. Included in this is an ability to recall what was necessary should the Jurisdiction require it.

Progression

Members Progress not on their ability to exemplify what they profess but upon their ability to remember and repeat back from each Performance what they are told to repeat back. The member must be ready, willing and able to support the system already in existence to Progress within it.

Although the information within each Performance is the overt focus for the Candidate, the Organization itself is only concerned with whether the Candidate remembers what he experienced well enough to repeat it back should he desire to become a supporting cast member.

Of course, many Jurisdictions now omit the need for any Candidate to learn and repeat back anything other than the Modes of Recognition, thus allowing them to enter the Lodge and participate in the simplest of Society activities.

Some Jurisdictions might require the Obligations to be repeated back. This emphasizes the need for members to be cognoscente of their Moral duties to God, themselves and the Society, with their fellow man being included in this last duty. It is unfortunate that even this is not required in all existing Freemasonic Societies.

Now more than ever, fewer and fewer Jurisdictions require the entire Script to be learned by Candidates. Learning the scripts allows each member to step into the role of any part required to support the Performances offered to the next Candidates. Without it, the member can't truly participate fully in what is offered him.

Because the Society has forgotten the original focus of the Craft, they have omitted this specific training activity among members. This is one of the central reasons the

Society itself is floundering. You can't reasonably expect a Society based upon Acting to maintain itself, much less grow, if Acting is no longer supported. It would be like expecting builders to build without proper plans, tools and materials. It can be done, but to what end?

Harmony

Members must continuously engage in activities Harmoniously. Disharmony is not tolerated.

In the early days of the Society, when there were any contentions between members, it was expected that the meeting was to be used to iron out these disagreements. Meetings were expected to continue until harmony was restored and all present were expected to stay until this occurred. As you might imagine, this created a huge incentive to employ peer pressure to minimize the time members would be held hostage to the contentions of others within meetings. It also meant members would not attend if they knew in advance there were contentions that would hold them to longer meeting times then they had planned.

To prevent this, rules were rewritten and men who had issues with each other could prevent the other from attending with a simple approval from the main officer.

Additionally, the sources of contention, primarily the issues surrounding politics and religion were proscribed from discussion during meetings. As a result, contentious discourse within the meetings was minimized. Harmony was therefore and thereon an established and legally supported standard of operations.

Anything that didn't support the Harmony of Organization and therefore might interfere with its primary purpose of performing its Morality based plays would not be tolerated.

Status Quo

Members must accept and support well-established systems and resist any desire to change things, unless the entire Organization has already stated the change is required. Should any one member even suggest a change to the system, ample societal pressures are employed to maintain the status quo. This is paramount and requires the consideration and implementation of removal of the member should there be any possibility that the member might rally support for his suggestion.

Only changes that are absolutely required due to outside influences upon the Organization are to be considered and even those are to be considered over many years to assure that no other response would suffice.

This is quite evident from the Society's history. Bending to legal and cultural pressures has slowly modified even the Landmarks adopted by many Jurisdictions, especially within the USA. Public events that have raised outcries from non-members have caused changes in Society operations that are still in existence decades and centuries later.

It's most unfortunate that both members and non-members alike don't realize that the Society itself is merely practicing Privatized Theater that offers its members total immersion into Morality plays that emphasizes Moral Responsibility. So much contention would be removed if the façade were to be acknowledged up front *before* the masks are applied.

Purposefulness

One purpose of the Society is to render an interesting and intriguing blend of Miracle and Morality plays whose primary intent is to introduce men to Moral thought and being. It currently employs this introduction by way of Total Immersion Theater where Candidates are asked to embrace the part they play, to do so without reservation and to use it as a rule and guide to their further moral development.

It is brilliant in its construction and when rendered well, it pulls Candidates into each play's reality seamlessly. Individuals who experience these plays may go to their death never realizing in what they had actually participated.

Getting Honest

Unfortunately, Candidates are not told this upfront. They are led to believe that what is offered is based upon fact, not allegory. Candidates and members alike never realize that they are part of a play and that all that unfolds is exactly what they choose. The whole rendering is done so mechanically that even the existing members don't realize what is truly going on and fall victim to an all encompassing virtual reality where all who are involved believe that they are what they are instructed to profess.

An Unwanted Winnowing

Furthermore, should the Society continue to mindlessly reenact, continue to misunderstand its origins and continue to employ the façade unknowingly, Craft degradation shall continue. Huge numbers of members shall continue to leave disappointed, disillusioned and disgruntled. Those that remain shall continue as Patrons, support the system financially but not knowing what is actually being supported or believe that they are supporting something totally different than it truly is. A few shall continue to step up to support the system of Degree Performances with time and energy, dedicated to support theatrical productions not knowing its underlying purposes.

Should things continue as they are, there shall not be enough members to make a long term difference. The cultures surrounding the Society today are not ones to provide unsophisticated Candidates. Not many new Candidates will willingly engage in such activities. Today's Candidates want continuity between the act and the reality it is supposed to improve.

More and more Candidates want to know the true basis for their invitation. More and more shall leave when they realize that what they have joined is no more than just a superficial introduction to Mysteries not supported by the theatrical productions offered. Without such backing and upfront honesty, Candidates shall continue to join and then leave when they discover otherwise.

If only someone could communicate clearly to existing members and future members the Craft's origin, its current methods and the Morality that these methods are intended to convey. Perhaps the Light would allow for men to better understand what they are actually doing, rather than just accepting the many masks that they are asked to wear.

Perhaps being consciously aware of this specific Light and discussing it between members could also make a significant difference for the better, to the Society's future, and its members.

XII. The Society of Entitlements

When all you're doing is Making Promises, Bestowing Titles and Memorizing and Reciting Scripts can you Honestly feel comfortable knowing that nothing of true Value is being offered beyond these activities.

It is clear that all that is espoused within the Society is not fully practiced. The Scripts it uses to help convey Moral teachings are brilliant. The Work it directs us to do is life changing. The manner to which it has preserved these scripts is inspiring. The commitment it has inspired to support its Grand and Important Undertaking rivals those rendered by history's greatest leaders. The Society's one major failing is the little to no emphasis it places upon supporting the very Work toward which its Rituals direct its members.

It should not surprise anyone who understands the Craft, why it only supports actor development. The entirety of its Performances depends upon a well-trained and dedicated troop of actors. Those who learn the scripts eventually progress through to the next level, and they are entitled as such. A member who learns the script of the

Entered Apprentice Performance is entitled to progress to the next level. That member is also entitled to play a role in any Entered Apprentice Degree that is performed within their Lodge and possibly their Jurisdiction, depending upon the rules of their Grand Lodge. They become valuable members in that they can now support the machine that is the Blue Lodge, at the first level.

Moreover, it does not stop there. The same conditions are applied to the Fellow Craft Degree Performance. Should a member experience the second Degree, and learn the scripts, they can engage in supporting the Lodge's efforts to put on that Degree. As a Fellow Craft, all that this title can afford a member is there for the taking.

Furthermore, should a member go through the Master Mason Degree, and learn the Degree scripts, he is entitled to all that the title allows.

Title Bound

It is really important to understand that the meaning placed upon each title has truly nothing to do with their scripted references. A Society Apprentice truly does not serve a suitable time as an Apprentice, learning the Craft that the Degree espouses. All that is required is that he learns his part and do it well enough to support the next Candidates to come through at that level.

Each Candidate should be required to do what the first Degree espouses. He should be held to a standard that requires him to establish and maintain:

1) A firm understanding as to what it truly Important to him in life.
2) A firm understanding of his current and desired future Morality.

3) A workable system that supports the development and cultivation of Values.
4) A workable system that supports the development and Cultivation of Priorities.
5) A workable Time Management system.
6) A workable system that supports the development and cultivation of Standards and Boundaries
7) A workable Emotional Management system.
8) A workable system supporting divestiture of Vices and Superfluities.
9) A workable system that develops and cultivates Virtues within himself.
10) A workable system that supports the development and cultivation of Integrity.

Of course, all of this is not required since the Society places its support solely upon the Performance of the scripts and not what the Scripts direct members toward. If you can verbally draw the Entered Apprentice Degree map, you can then progress within the Organization. It doesn't matter to the Society if you can follow the map or not. It only matters that you can render it well enough to teach the next Candidate coming through how to verbally draw it for himself.

Likewise, this same condition exists for both the Fellow Craft and Master Mason Level. If you were to be held accountable for what the Fellow Craft Degree espouses, you would be required to learn the Seven Liberal Arts & Sciences well enough to teach them to those who want to learn them for themselves.

To put this into perspective, you would have to learn the lexicon (vocabulary), rule base and application of:

1) Grammar – Symbols as Words & Language.
2) Logic – Symbols as Premises and Arguments.

3) Rhetoric – Symbols as Figures of Speech and Constructs.
4) Arithmetic – Symbols as Numbers.
5) Geometry – Symbols as Numbers in Space.
6) Music – Symbols as Numbers in Time.
7) Astronomy – Symbols as Numbers in Space & Time.

Furthermore, if you were to be held to Account for what the Master Mason Level conveys, you would be required to have created a Masterpiece that is recognized and accepted as such by other Masters and to Masterfully apply and teach all that is espoused within the first two Degrees scripts, not just the scripts themselves.

The Reality

Freemasonic Blue Lodge Degree Titles mean that the member holding it has learned the Blue Lodge scripts well enough to step into the role the Society needs to assure the parts in the play are supported for the next Candidate coming through. No Apprenticeship is truly served. No Fellow Craft abilities are developed and cultivated. No Mastery is truly obtained, other than rendering a script for the Society plays when the Lodge needs them.

It's most unfortunate that the Society never developed itself beyond the roles it asks its members to act out. Had it taken what its scripts espouse to the next level, and provided authentic and functional support to its members in achieving what its Rituals have pointed its members toward, its membership and its surrounding structure would indeed be far grander than what is currently presented.

XIII. The First Freemason

When you follow the Trail long enough,
you might come to a Clearing.

When you consider everything about the Freemasonic
Society as it exists today and all that it does to Progress its
members, it becomes apparent what the Craft actually is.
With research, it takes some effort to back track in time to
discover who the first Freemason actually was.

If I were to read the heading, *The First Freemason,*
within the table of contents, I would find myself being
compelled to jump to that section first and eagerly read it. I
would get so excited about something that I wanted to
know that I would read ahead and discover spoilers that
would ruin the beginning of the book.

It's for that exact reason that I shall not start off telling
you about the first Freemason. I shall however initially
provide you some amusement by revealing a very
fascinating and innovative guy who practiced an interesting
and entertaining Craft. This distracting act of mine will
hopefully remind you that if you dared to read ahead and

not read the previous chapters that lead up to and support this one you shall ruin the intended experience by not setting the proper Foundation.

If you recall, the Performance that is called *Ritual* did not allow you to jump ahead. You had to experience it from its beginning to have the effect that its writers desired you to have. It is the same with this chapter and so I hope that you shall fully honor what is being shared.

So, with that being said, and with the implied assurance from you that you have read the previous chapters, let us first discuss an entirely different Craft figure to set the tone for what is to come.

Ancient Greece

The date was sometime around 534 BCE. I use the word *around* because the calendar has changed so many times since that point in history that the exact date is difficult to ascertain. No one really knows for sure because in all honesty, it's so close to Time Immemorial that for all intents and purposes, it might as well be.

It was during this century that the establishment of western theatrical tradition occurred. Spurred on by the annual festivals featuring ritual coral dances honoring Dionysius, the god of wine and fertility, it is said that these activities were the beginning of tragic drama and acting. It was at this moment in history, in ancient Greece during the sixth century BCE, that a ruler by the name of Peisistratus[50] had introduced a competitive contest at the Dionysian festival in Athens.

Up until then, all performances involved choral renderings of song and dance. The songs were always narratives that communicated in the third person and were rendered in group fashion.

Stepping Out

But an innovative man by the name of Thespis[51] chose to do something different for the competition held that year. According to what Aristotle is reported to have said[52], nearly two hundred years later, Thespis was one of the singers in the choral who sang dithyrambs. These were songs about stories that were based upon the accepted religions of the time and which had choric refrains as part of the song structure. At this competition, Thespis introduced an entirely different form of performance. He dared to step out from the group, be an individual and, cloaked in nothing more than a mask of a character, render the first documented case of staged impersonation.

At this juncture in time, the singer, poet and playwright departed from the traditional choral performance and introduced a solo performer who donned the persona of another individual and spoke as if he were that individual, assisted by the choral. It was through Thespis' action that was created the first act where story telling became a personal experience between the audience and an individual purposefully portraying someone else.

At first it was merely one solo performer, a protagonist, who was assisted by a chorus and leader. Many separate masks were used during the performance. With time and further innovations, these masks were eventually removed, since many different enhancing paints and textures were applied directly to the skin and surrounding areas to replace them. But this would not occur for some time.

In the meantime, with further experimentation, other actors were also added to these performances and the face of theater was transformed. The poet Aeschylus was to add a second character, a deuterogonist, and Sophocles a third, a tritagonist. Characters in opposition to the protagonist and other players, the antagonists, were also added. As more and more actors took the stage, the importance of the chorus eventually diminished.

Capitalizing on his success, Thespis also invented theatrical touring.[53] He did this by touring various cities while carrying his costumes, masks and other props in a horse-drawn wagon.[54]

Vying for a Goat

It should be noted here that the Greek style Tragedy was originally associated with winning a prize goat, according to some scholars. A goat was offered to winners of choral competitions for outstanding performances. This is further confirmed by the Roman poet Quintus Horatius Flaccus, also known as *Horace.* In his writing *Epistulae, he* refers to participants in these competitions as those *"Carmino qui tragico vilem certavit ob hircum"* which translates to *"Who in tragic song competed for a he-goat".* [55] Additionally, tragedies have been associated with the ritual sacrifice of animals around which choruses danced prior to these sacrifices[56].

It is speculated that Thespis was awarded such a prize when he was the first one to win a Tragic Competition. The word root of *Tragedy* originally meant, "he-goat ode[g]".

---

[g] It derives from Classical Greek τραγῳδία, contracted from trag(o)-aoidiā = "goat song", which comes from tragos = "he-goat" and aeidein = "to sing" (cf. "ode").

The Actors

With the success of Thespis, this specific type of acting soon became a recognizable and sought after art form. Actors became those societal individuals who were expected to convincingly portray a character in a dramatic or comic production. They received their name from the Greek word, ὑποκριτής (hypokrites), literally *means "one who interprets"* [57]. Their Craft renderings might be *Presentational* or *Representational* in forms. The former refers to a relationship between the actor and audience, whether by direct address or indirectly, by specific use of language, looks, gestures or other signs that indicate the "in character" actor is aware of the audience's presence. The later style refers to full submersion into the character when, *"actors want to make us 'believe' they are the character; they pretend."* [58]

From early times, actors were viewed with general distrust. Formerly, in some societies, only men could become actors because it was viewed to be a far worse disgrace for females to work the Craft. It was not until the 19th and 20th century CE that society had a reversal of opinion about actors.

Fast Forward

Even though actors in general were not thought of very highly for what they did up until the fall of the Roman Empire, Tragedies and Comedies were still enjoyed immensely. With that fall also came a far greater negative attitude upon those who would practice the Craft of theater from the Roman Catholic Church. With the Church's influence, actors were deemed unsuitable for Christian burials and therefore forever condemned. Many were not permitted entry into some towns and cities.

It was not until about 900 CE, when the Church began its quest to bring their message to the ignorant masses through Miracle-Saint plays. At first the plays were within the confines of the church and limited to the clergy. Soon they were taking place in the open and with the assistance of actors outside the clergy. They sought out actors for their skills to assist in that effort. The Church's shift in attitude toward actors showed that the Craft was not so disgraceful after all. That is, as long as it was used to help support the Church's efforts to bring its message to the masses.

Of course, within a very few centuries, the church all but extricated itself from its Miracle/Saint plays it originally brought to the masses. This left the job to be performed by the guilds who continued to use these and other plays types to entertain the general public while educating them on scripture, Morals and their product and service offerings.

The First

This leads us back to the whole point of this chapter. You are already aware from your reading of the connection between acting and the Guild performances called *Mystery Plays*. You are also aware of how they eventually led to what is practiced today by Freemasons all around the world.

What was provided by this chapter were the pieces of the puzzle that remained hidden for three hundred years. The connection of Freemasonry with the goat was one piece. The exclusion of females from the Premier Grand Lodge was another. The extensive memory work that remained the primary mode of Progression was a third. All are explained by understanding how Thespis created the Craft, how it developed over the years and ultimately lead

116

to how the Freemasonry Craft is Practiced within the Society today.

Please consider for a moment what occurred in ancient Greece and the innovation of just one man that made possible the very activities that are now known as Freemasonry. When you do, it should be clear to you by now who the first Freemasonic Craft Practitioner actually was.

A Final Note to Goat Riders

As I was writing this, I could not help to think about the term that so many members have used to tease third Degree Candidates as they are preparing for their experience. Freemasons have used the term "riding the goat" for many years now. It's unfortunate that contrary to what is popularly believed about *"Riding the Goat"* originating as a Freemasonic term, its origins appear to come from an anonymous expose attack upon the Odd Fellows organization that was first published in 1845 CE.[59] I say unfortunate because it perfectly fits with Freemasonic origins.

Let's take a look at this closely.

As I researched this chapter and as I have already written, I found that the Word *"Tragedy"* came from Greek roots that meant *"he-goat ode"*. They were initially choral competitions where the prize was a goat and that they may have involved sacrifice. Over time, Tragedy became known more for the actual performances

than any associated sacrifice or prize. To experience them, to actually be carried through these tragedies as a cast member, especially for the first time, must have been quite an experience indeed.

This same experience of Tragedy occurs for the first time for Freemasonic Candidates, who are carried through the third Degree Tragedy by their Brothers' Performances. Little do these Candidates and supporting cast members realize that to *"Ride the Goat"* is to experience firsthand a play styled after a Greek Tragedy. Just like back then, there is sacrifice and the hope of reward. This is exactly what each Candidate experience by being carried through the third Degree Tragedy by their more experienced theatrical Brothers.

The Point within a Circle

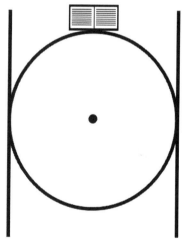

There's yet another interesting Freemasonic connection to Thespis that I had not known about until I did this research. Many years ago, I did some intense investigation into the Circumpunct. At that time I learned some interesting things about the symbol and how it was connected to so many Freemasonic references.

As many members of the Fraternity have seen it, the Circumpunct appears flanked by two parallel lines. A holy book is often seen flanking the top of the circle midway between the two parallel lines. It is referred to within Ritual as *the Point within a Circle flanked by two perpendicular parallel lines.* Members are told that, as men and members of the Society, Candidates are the point within the circle. Many members are told so while being surrounded by their Brothers. Furthermore, they are told to circumscribe their desires and keep their passions within due bounds. It is indeed a powerful reminder to all those who understand its significance to the Ritual they experience.

However, is it also a reminder of Thespis. Let me explain.

The Arena Stage

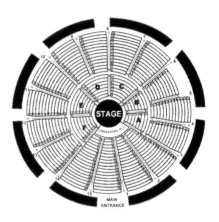

The Arena Stage, also known as *"Theater-in-the-round, central stage; centre stage theatre; island stage",* form of theater comes from ancient roots. The acting area is completely surrounded by the audience and is either raised or at floor level. It has been theorized that the informality thus established leads to increased rapport between the audience and the actors.

The Arena Stage has its roots in ancient Greece where the rituals performed eventually evolved into classical Greek theatre. During medieval times, especially in England, it was used once again. It eventually fell into less use as the open stage of Elizabethan times became preferred. Eventually, the proscenium stage came to dominate theatre during the late 17th century CE. This stage limited audiences to the area directly in front of the stage.

The Point within a Circle is clearly evident in the Arena Stage.

Theta is for Thespis

It is however the first letter of the name of the first Freemason that has perhaps the most telling of all symbols used within the Freemasonic Lodge. I came across this bit of well hidden Light while researching the symbol of Salt, one of four wages[60] provided to the builders of Solomon's temple. The symbol that I found for salt was a circle with a horizontal line dividing it in one half "⊖".

While searching for salt's symbol, I came across the symbol for Theta also. There were several ways that the symbol for Theta was expressed. One way was identical to that which was used for salt. Two other forms were archaic. In the ancient form, Theta was written as a cross or plus sign within a circle that touches the inner part of each circle. Later renderings of Theta were as a circle with a line within it (Θ) or, much later, a point within a circle (⊙).

And it was that last rendering of Theta, the point within a circle, which caught my interest immediately. There, hidden in plain sight in many Lodges scattered around the globe was the first letter of the first Freemason's name *Thespis* in Greek – Θέσπις!

Only most members would not recognize it because it's entirely Greek to them.

120

XIV. Freemasonry 101

The Basics of Freemasonry are clear. To fit in, you must know your part.

The Craft focuses upon conveying Moral Principles and teachings through Allegory and Symbols to those Patrons who step up and volunteer to experience its Performances. In addition to this, they only allow into the Society those who are already morally good men who are well recommended. The experience comes with conditions and those conditions bind those who go through it not just remain good but to Become Better.

The object of the training that is offered by the Freemasonic Society to those who follow through on their Obligations is to learn the words, signs and grips used during the Performance. Members who come from Jurisdictions that recognizes the significance of remembering the words that were used to bind men to Become Better are required to remember and recite the Obligations too. The Jurisdictions that know how important it is to learn the Craft and not just the Morality that members are supposed to bind themselves to, also require members to memorize and recite back more. This task is extensive and includes the actual step by step events that each went through during his first experience of the Performance and to within a reasonably acceptable precision.

Once again, it is not ever emphasized that any member understands anything that he memorizes and repeats. It is never emphasized that he must do any of the work which any of what he is memorizing points toward. He need not understand the lessons. He need not understand what the Symbols mean or toward what work they direct his attention. He is not even required to discuss how he can use what he is told to memorize to Better himself. It is only important that he be able to memorize and recite back what is asked of him by his Jurisdiction. And that is exactly what is supported by his society as a whole.

If you haven't heard this enough and have yet to understand what all this means, let me spell it out for you. This is exactly what actors are trained to do. They are only required to memorize a script and recite it back as required. It is one of many skills necessary to put on a Performance and Freemasonic training within the Blue Lodge level is exactly this – *Actor Training*.

The Mask

You might ask yourself, *"If Freemasonic Training is based upon actor development and cultivation, what exactly is this supposed to do for members?"* And this is a very good question to ask because it gets to the core of what Freemasonry actually is.

When you take the mask off of Freemasonry and realize that it is an acting based society, you might begin to understand why it supports what it does.

More specifically, Freemasonry is a Theatrical Society that uses the Mask of Stonecraft as applied to the Spiritual Building of Good men to direct them toward Moral

Betterment and gives them ample Opportunity to Commit to that Betterment.

Little Known Perks

There are obvious benefits to the current Freemasonic training that requires memorization of these scripts beyond being able to perform the Scripts. Bonding time between Brothers occurs for those who take advantage of it. Development of what the Greeks called *Artificial Memory* within the Parietal and Occipital lobes of the brain occurs. And the most important perk of all, the installation within a man of three Morality-based road maps which he can follow at any time to direct and correct his behavior toward Betterment.[61] From that moment on, it is the responsibility of each member to Travel the roads these maps reveal to them and do so with unwavering zeal.

XV. The Grand Conspiracy

So much has been lost to time; too much in fact.

If all the governments and all the institutions that condemned and ban the Society of Free & Accepted Masons from their domains only knew how insane their fears were, they would never be tempted to accuse the Society of anything other than making effort to entertain good men and give opportunity to them to become better in all facets of their lives.

For nearly three hundred years libraries have been filled with the carefully crafted imaginings of Freemasonic histories. From its beginnings, its efforts to keep their plays private have caused individuals, institutions and governments to imagine the worst. Accusations of subterfuge, intrigue and deception continue to be placed upon the Society to this day. Conspiracy theorists profit by keeping these imaginings alive in the minds of fundamentally mistrusting individuals and they fuel the obsessed with wilder and more far reaching claims. Sheer stupidity keeps such rumors circulating in and around the cloistered forums, chat rooms and blogs. Each feeds off the fears created and each are fueled by ignorance.

The Society also benefits by all the efforts of those who would portray it in ugly, unfavorably or disturbing light. Many a man has been drawn by the distortions and projections by those who would do harm to the Society into investigating the Society trying to see what was behind the accusations. Most of the brightest of them come to understand what the Society has to truly offer and join soon thereafter, enjoying the rights, lights and benefits that only an association with it can bring. Had they known from the beginning of their search that it would reveal something grander than they could ever have imagined, perhaps they would have investigated the Organization sooner.

Time Honored Traditions

Even though some modern day religious leaders don't realize the Society of Free & Accepted Masons is a theatrical based organization, they have opted to condemn Freemasons and their Organization without realizing that they are continuing in a long standing tradition themselves.

Throughout the Middle Ages, religious leaders routinely condemned actors and their profession. As one author put it:

"...the clergy were uncompromising opponents of theatrical amusement in any shape. They reprehended play-going as incompatible with true devotion, purity of life and sobriety of thought. They condemned the actor to a kind of social outlawry, declaring that, unless he solemnly forswore his profession, he could not receive the Holy Communion or be entitled to Christian burial." [62]

These condemnations occurred throughout that time and even before. Today, there are many within the clergy who condemn Freemasonry and its members along the very same lines. Little does either side know that this condemnation started shortly after the fall of the Roman Empire with the condemnation of its theatrical troops.

Another Tradition

Clergy members are not the only ones who have their strong opinions and traditions. Freemasonry as a Theatrical Society also employs one clearly evident long standing tradition that is very closely associated with its theatrical roots and was influenced by clergy's attitudes from early on. That tradition is one that bans the inclusion of females within its ranks.

Many members of the Freemasonic society do not know that it was illegal in many parts of Europe and other locations around the world for females to participate on stage in any theatrical productions until the 17th century CE. Until that time, the culture and mores of the times led people to believe it to be disgraceful for a female to participate in this Craft.

When you consider Freemasonic Theatrical roots, it becomes clear that the Society continued this tradition and even incorporated it into their rules once the Society started to grow. It is a fact that such formal exclusion of women from the Society did not officially occur until Brother Anderson proscribed them from the Society of Free & Accepted Masons in his writing efforts to legitimize the Craft[63]. Up until that time, there was no such prescription and similar Craft productions did include females, although their inclusion was rare.

Further Condemnations

Considering these theatrical roots, it becomes a disturbing irony that Freemasonry would be outlawed in any way. Yet, the ignorance of many leaders who outlaw the Craft from being practiced within their borders is a compliment and testament to the illusion that Freemasonic efforts bring forth. Freemasons have done such a superb portrayal of its plays and principles and what they stand for that even outsiders are fooled into believing the reality Freemasonry makes effort to create.

The Only Secret

Should they observe the Society very closely, they would have to admit that the Organization's only secret was a universal agreement among its members to partake in a benevolent worldwide  conspiracy. That sole conspiracy is to entice men into taking an honest and fearless look at their morals. Included in that enticement is an invitation to have each of them commit to become Better men for their efforts.

And all of this was to be accomplished through the Total Immersion of each man in to a Live Action Role Playing (LARP) designed around the Symbolic Application of Stonecraft. All who Enter the Society, Pass through its Rituals and eventually Rise to the occasion agree to make their very best efforts to portray authentically and to their best ability, the Character of a Worthy Grand Master.

This means as Freemasons (Organizational members) they adopt the façade of Speculative Masons to Build their Personal Character and do so through the Theater of the Lodge, within and without.

It is shear genius in its simplicity and quite Masterful in its renderings!

XVI. Craft Ramifications

Facing the Challenge that Chasing Masonic Rabbits has brings forth many associated problems and troubles. Take care in the Rabbits you chase for snares are everywhere.

All this information puts the Craft in a much different Light. Up until now, many of the theories that have been put forth and entertained by both serious scholars and casual members have assumed that the Craft was a continuation of any one of many possibilities. Here are a few that have been put forth in the past:

1) Some form or another of a continuation of a Builder type organization.
2) An Ancient Initiatic Society.
3) An organization formed in Time Immemorial.
4) Some sort of Religious Sect.
5) Some sort of Secret Society.

But understanding its true origins and its true Practice enables members to see more clearly what the Craft actually is.

Freemasonry

The Cloak of Freemasonry is worn by millions of its members. It is an Initiatic society in the truest sense in that its primary focus is to Initiate (Make; Accept) members. It also maintains the organizational structure and operations to assure that this sole function continues unchecked and unaltered. There are auxiliary operations and structures that are offshoots of the primary organization but its primary focus always takes priority.

Because of this, almost all Freemasonic Blue Lodge Education focuses upon either Initiation training (three levels) or Officer training (running the Lodge). The former involves both Candidates going through the Initiations and the Initiation teams responsible for assuring the Initiation Process is adhered to without wavering. The latter involves the line officers responsible for maintaining the building, and associated property, operations and maintenance. Sometimes these two educational focuses overlap depending upon who's involved.

Occasionally there might be some other education topics offered dealing with Freemasonic history, laws, tradition, etiquette, and associated Organization topics but they are information based rather than actual training.

The primary Freemasonic Educational focus however almost always deals with organizational rather than member support.

The Skin of Masonry

Under the cloak of Freemasonry exists the skin of Masonry. Masonry, as it is described by Freemasonic Rituals used throughout most USA Jurisdictions, is the Progression of its members from Youth, to Adulthood and finally to Age. It is not the Rituals themselves or the Society that conveys them. It is the Practice of what they point men toward and it is conveyed as instruction sets.

The instruction sets laid out by Ritual are intended to develop and cultivate those who follow it. It is believed that following them eventually brings forth Wisdom, Beauty and Strength from within each member. The goal of this Work is to make sure that each of these three qualities are present within members and that they are in harmony with each other. The end result of the Work Betters individuals, especially by strengthening their Moral Foundation and Awareness.

There is currently no widespread Masonic Training offered by the Cloaking Organization. All Masonic Training is left up to the individuals who desire to develop and cultivate themselves.

Craft Muscle

When the skin of Masonry is taken off, it reveals the supporting muscle that assists in the delivery of the message. You see the true Art and Craft of Freemasonry. *Without a doubt the Art and Craft is Theater.* Proficiencies are all acting-centric; from the memorization of scripts to the pronunciation of specific words. Chorography is included in this. All of this supports the Ceremonial plays that must be acted out to perfection to assure the paying Patrons coming through are pulled into the world the Lodge makes effort to create, just for them.

Unfortunately, far too many members of the Society fail to understand what they are actually doing. They go through the motions prescribed by the long established traditions of the Society truly believing that these plays are actually ancient Rituals. They don't realize that they are putting on a theatrical Performance. They also fail to understand the results that are intended by their supportive actions.

The Core

Going deeper, past the muscle and into the core, you reach the very center of which the entire Organization revolves. That Core is Morality. From its very beginning, through the Middle Ages and into present day, Morality is what the Craft was intended to Better.

This Core is not what many within the Craft focus upon though. Many would rather experience flights of fancy having to do with all to which Rituals allude rather than the Morality its Practice should bring forth. This is understandable. The Core can be a frightening thing to explore for it requires men to face their own Morality and that is something many men avoid at all costs. It takes a very special soul to venture into this territory. Not many men approach it, much less embrace and improve it.

It would be grand if the Society put together support for this Betterment.

Craft Disgrace

When you consider that all Candidates are paying hard earned money to experience a believable top

notch Performance, it is with the utmost disappointment that anyone, Candidate or member, must witness any Performance as less than authentic. Too many members performing these Degrees break from their character and reveal the man behind the mask.

To stay true to the Craft, members must remember that Candidates are first and foremost paying Patrons. Their money supports the Lodge. In no way should their experience of the Performance be tainted by members revealing the actors behind the masks. The instant a performer breaks character they ruin what is being portrayed. This occurs by:

1) making unscripted side comments to another cast member.
2) making light of his portrayal by using body language that reflects his personal attitude toward what he is doing rather than the attitude that must be portrayed by his character.
3) making humorous gestures or comments to other cast members that are out of character.
4) *"playing"* to the other cast members rather than to the audience he was supposed to pla*y – The Candidate!*

    It is a serious a breach of the Craft to do any of these during a Ritual Performance. It is an offense to the Craft to not bar these members, as well-intentioned as they are, from ever performing again, until, that is, they can show that they have mended their ways.

Lost in the Metaphor

    On the other hand, membership in the Freemasonic Society is not without its challenges. Many members immerse themselves so deeply into the culture and role playing that they actually lose themselves forever in the mythology of the Society. Some may use it as a way of fulfilling deeply seated control issues that play out in the climb through the many layers of authority that have grown with the Society. Others use it as a way of obtaining a license to worship without the baggage associated with many religious structures surrounding their chosen Faith.

    Whatever the reason or need, Freemasonry presents many venues and provides to those who embrace it a multitude of possibilities. It is truly important for all members to get real about what they are trying to accomplish by all these activities and *make them-selves Better men by their collective and personal efforts!*

XVII. Refocusing the Craft

Masonic Masks Compel men toward
Playing Major Life-Changing Roles for Real.

By lifting away Freemasonry's Curtain, you find behind it the man that Freemasonic Scripts Allude to and who the Craft makes effort to build. He is not a Speculative Stoneworker. He is not a man masquerading as a Ritual obsessed manikin. He is not a prudish preservationist of inconsequential Tradition. He is a man possessed by the Spirit of God, driven to be Moral unto death and who sees no difference between the belief that he professes and who he truly is.

He calls himself a Mason, but he is Built up of Moralities few men shall ever know.

Improving a man doesn't occur instantaneously. Developing such Masonic Disciplines requires first the ordering of his heart, then the ordering of his mind, and lastly, that of his spirit! Before he is able to do any of this for himself, he must first commit to being someone he is not. It is the only way to become someone who he is not already.

In Character

In this respect, the number one rule that any Performing member must adhere to respect the Craft and its members is: *never break character, ever!* Once the Performance has begun, all cast members must be in Character from then on.

You might believe that the demarcation between when to be in Character and when to be yourself is clear. You might also assume that any one Performance begins when the Lodge is opened. And you'd be right, but you'd be missing the whole point of the Society.

The Performance doesn't start at the opening of Lodge. The Performance doesn't even begin once you enter the Lodge building. You must always remember that the Performance is based upon *the reality that is embraced by the Society,* not the start of any one meeting. Thus, the Performance, *your Performance,* begins even before you ask for a petition. If your Character is not already what the Society accepts, you had better reconsider your efforts.

Representation

Current members should remember who they represent. As members of the Society, they represent what the Craft does. Not what it can do. Not what it should do. But what it actually does!

Candidates are seeking to join the Society. They want to know that what they are joining is right for them. They want to see what they are joining through the portrayals of the existing members.

When you don't realize that

this is a Performance Society, you are likely to forget that you are always being viewed by the All Seeing Eye of society as a whole. This includes and is not limited to your fellow Brothers, your family, your friends, your neighbors and your coworkers. Through *who you are* every last one of them sees who you portray yourself to be. If you are putting on an inauthentic act, your very looks shall betray you. They shall soon see you for who you truly are. You must actually become the part you play and you are on stage around the clock and even in the privacy of your own home.

Total Emersion

Creating a space where the outside world cannot interfere is a time honored tradition for anyone who seeks more than what the outside world could possible offer. The central power of the Freemasonic Society is the mutual agreement of all its members to play the part inside and

outside of the Lodge. This means that the entire world is their theater and members are expected to play the part for the rest of their lives.

The Lodge is the perfect place to practice this. Within the Lodge you have an opportunity to practice what is taught through the Ritual plays. General meetings offer activities which you may engage in that allow for further cultivation of what is espoused within Ritual Performances.

Safe Harbor

Perhaps the greatest service Freemasonic Society can ever offer a man is the ability to release himself from the everyday world and immerse himself in a reality that offers him fellowship that's not contingent upon anything other than wanting to be together for all the right reasons. In this way, Ritual does indeed *Bring Order to Chaos.*

Moreover, Freemasonry is perhaps the single most inclusive way for any man to freely and willingly immerse himself within a nurturing environment of Moral instruction that excludes the varying degrees of politically corrupting influences of any one religion.

Furthermore, there are some deeply spiritual men who shall never ever step foot in any religion based facility who desire to commune with other Seekers of like Mind and Spirit. For them there is and shall always be Freemasonry.

And all members reap the benefit of their presence and wisdom as a result.

XVIII.   The Play on The Word

*From the Perspective of
Freemasonic Practice, the
Master's Word is Played out
every time a Member Portrays
Masonry Authentically.*

    The search for the lost Master's Word
has been waved as a carrot before Freemasonic Society
members from the moment the third Degree was created in
its current form. It was a brilliant change to the original
Freemasonic plays since it left members wanting more and
eager to invest more time, energy and money seeking to
obtain it. This one word has been the focus of countless
conjectures and some very deep speculations. To draw
members into further societal involvements, this word
search was used strategically as leverage. It has even been
offered for fee by Degrees outside the Blue Lodge Theater.
Yet, examining the actual Craft that is both Practiced and
supported by the Society today, it should be clearly evident
what The Word actually is.

    You can take many directions in making effort to solve
one of the greatest of Freemasonic mysteries ever created
by the Craft, that is, next to its origins and who was the first
Freemason. You can join other branches of the Society
which claim to provide it. You can comb the various on-
line resources that are available in abundance that offer to
you The Word as it is shared within these Performances.
You can even fossick through Rituals both current and past
to try to gather clues and to solve the puzzle for yourself.

No matter what you do there shall never be anyone who shall reach out, shake your hand and say, "you got it", *unless you truly are It.* It is most unfortunate that such imaginings fuel the activities of many members.

Once you understand what It actually is, you come to realize too that you cannot ever possess The Word. This is because The Word is not something you can hold, say or write. You cannot possess it in any way. If anything, *It must be something that possesses you and does so legitimately and authentically.* If all this sounds confusing to you, perhaps reassessing what you have been told might help you better grasp what The Word actually is.

Let's take another look at the requirements that point to all this in Ritual.

Ineffable

It is implied through Freemasonic Ritual and Lore that the Master's Word is ineffable. It is clear that the meaning of the word *ineffable* does not mean that it will not or shall not be shared through written or auditory transmission because of some agreement or desire. It means it cannot be shared these ways because it is impossible to do so. This is confirmed several times by one of the main character's statements to those who pursued him to take it from him. Even though he made every effort to let them know for what they were asking was impossible, they themselves could not begin to Grasp how true his words actually were.

The story is a brilliant illustration too, especially for those who view or experience it. The third Degree portrayal sets up a paradox for Patrons who make effort to understand this at its most superficial level.

Most people understand that words by their very nature are communicated orally or through writing. The question that arises immediately is: *If it cannot be communicated in this manner, then how does one obtain it?*

The question can only be answered by realizing first and foremost that The Word is not a word in its usual sense. Since all that is presented within Ritual is allegory, even The Word is Symbolic for something else.

The Word is a Metaphor. It is intended to represent something other than an actual word. To understand this metaphor, one must seek not what is communicated in its normal sense but to seek the *character* of what is communicated *beyond the words used.* Hence, to seek an actual word would be foolish, but to seek the character of The Word would be wise.

In this way it becomes clear why The Word is Ineffable. It lets the seeker know up front that he must not seek the answer in any superficial way.

Three must be Present

The most common mistake made by Society members who seek The Word is to believe that three people must be present to reveal it. Those who believe this forget that the whole third Degree dramatization is an allegorical play, not a historical recreation. This means that no one character portrayed by the play is actually a real person and none of the events that are portrayed really occurred. This includes the main character and supporting characters.

The whole idea behind the third Degree allegory is to motivate those who experience and examine it to think beyond the superficial characters portrayed within it. It is also a test to see if the Candidate understands that it is an allegory. Far too many members get swept away by the realism portrayed by the Degree team performing the allegory. Some actually start to believe it's a re-enactment of something that is history based. Some get so captivated by the Performance that they forget that the only thing that is portrayed is allegory in a highly stylized theater and by very dedicated amateur actors.

Why Allegory

Allegories are the primary method used throughout mankind's history to successfully convey Theological, Philosophical and Moralistic principles, concepts and ideas[64]. When you want to communicate such things to others, allegory is a very effective way of doing so; especially when it might be shared with people who cannot understand it in any way other than superficial.

Allegories are also purposefully constructed to portray concepts and ideas in symbolic form. The characters of the third Degree drama are all symbolic for things that are far beyond their superficial portrayals. For many, the Three Grand Masters are masks for Wisdom, Strength and Beauty. The Fellow Crafts reflect the collective masks of Desire. Even the Ruffians, who team together to place demands upon The Builder, are masks for many differing concepts. Some say they represent youth, manhood and age. Others say they represent the demands of time, morality and completion. All these vary depending upon what they represent to those experiencing them.

Allegory reminds those who encounter it that everything and everyone portrayed by it is a superficial mask for something far deeper. When it is applied to the third Degree drama, it lets those who remember this that it is not who must be present, *but rather what!*

Agreement of Three

For The Word to be revealed, not only must three be *present,* but they must also *agree.* Far too many members assume that the three that must be present must somehow

represent the Three Grand Masters rather than what the three Grand Masters represent. Hence additional elaborate dramatizations were created to convey The Word where three Patrons are required to have The Word revealed each time the Degree is performed. Careful scrutiny of this non-Blue Lodge Degree reveals that there is no actual agreement being reached by the three Patrons. All that occurs is a Performance that is also allegorical, but not truly supportive of the premise of The Word that was supposedly lost.

Why Seek It?

If you take into consideration why The Word was sought, you begin to understand what motivated the characters of the third Degree drama and also those who seek it to this day. According to the Drama, the whole purpose for seeking The Master's Word was to allow for its possessor *to travel, work, earn, support and contribute masterfully.* If you go upon what is offered in Higher Degrees, you shall be led to believe that three people are required to reveal It. Along with this are revealed spoken words, which clearly breaks with the understanding that it is an ineffable word.

None of this makes sense. Who travels around with two other companions to find work? Who wants to be dependent upon two other people to render Masterpieces? Who is going to believe that by saying what is believed to be the Master's Word, that any uninitiated employer will hire someone and pay him Master's Wages?

When you want to run a simple test so as to assure that what you were given is The Word all you have to do is apply it toward the ends you desire. Simply try to use what you have been given *to travel, work, earn, support and contribute masterfully* and do so without the aid of any other person.

When you can accomplish all this and do so consistently, you are indeed what you proclaim – *A Master*. When you can't, you have something, but it isn't The Word; and neither are you a Master.

If it has not become clear as to what The Word actually is, try to put it in terms of skill development. You can teach it, develop it and finally cultivate it to a fine art; one that is indistinguishable from the person rendering it. However, it is still up to the person who is being taught to learn it, develop it and cultivate it for themselves.

This is why it is so crucial to understand that The Word cannot be given to anyone. It is something that a person *Becomes* as a result of diligently *applying Wisdom, Strength and Beauty in agreement to all he does. One does not possess The Word, One Becomes The Word; and does so through dedication and commitment of specific Work.*

The Word within the Craft

From what Freemasonry conveys to its members, The Word is built up with three specific things which must be present and all must be in agreement. The Characters that must be present and in agreement are the personifications of Wisdom, Strength and Beauty; they are not the people themselves.

Applying this to what is provided to members by its dramatic Performance, these would be:

1) King Solomon, who represents *Wisdom* within the Theatrical Triad. From an actor's point of view, this part encompasses:

Who the actor is to Be
Why the actor is to Be
Where the actor is to Be
When the actor is to Be

The Society rules, traditions, Obligations and etiquette dictate and regulate all of these with the expressed permission and cooperation of each member.

2) King Hiram, who represents *Strength* within the Theatrical Triad. From an actor's point of view, this part encompasses:

What the actor must Be.

This means *what* he is to say and do guided by the Script and Choreography which is provided to him by the Society. These guidelines are to be adhered to by members without wavering.

3) Hiram Abiff, who represents *Beauty,* as cunning craftsmanship, within the Theatrical Triad. From an actor's point of view, this part encompasses:

How the actor is to Be.

This means *how* he is to render his Work as provided to him by the Society and is adhered to by members without wavering.

When all three of the qualities of each are present and all three agree, what the actor renders is considered Masterful.

Evidence

You can see this in Freemasonic Work no matter what level you examine. It should be clear that those who Masterfully portray their Society's roles are supported most for their efforts. Whether it is Performing Proficiencies, Degree Roles, Instruction or Officer Roles that support the other Lodge, District or Grand Lodge functions, it is all the same. The Society considers Mastery to be the Performance of Roles that support its operations; no more and no less.

The Word as it relates to the Society is the flawless Performance of Societal Roles as dictated by its scripts. It is not however the Mastery toward which these scripts direct its members. That's an entirely different Word.

The Master's Word

The Master's Word (also known as *"The Lost Word"* and *"The Word"*) alluded to within Ritual is echoed by what the Society seeks from members. In the allegory, It was sought to enable men *to travel, work, earn, support and contribute masterfully.* All this was as possible for Masterful men do then as it is now. But it is not because of anything that they can ever obtain from others. It is only by way of what each man has obtained from himself.

The Word is *Excellence* from oneself to the Degree that one does all these things Masterfully. *The Word is a metaphor for Masterful Achievement.*

XIX. The Role of a Lifetime

Good Ritual is so Compelling that you lose yourself in It.
Great Ritual is so Compelling that you Find yourself in It
and become someone Better.

There is rarely anything more valuable to a man than for him to truly know what's best for him. When a man knows what's best and he really wants this for himself, he is more apt to take actions and do the Work that shall bring about his Betterment. The downside of this is that men who want the benefits of such Work without actually doing the Work, may devise systems that allow for the delivery of those benefits at the expense of others and themselves.

Freemasonry is a culture that embraces purposeful and carefully fabricated realities brought about by highly stylized theatrical productions. They are replete with Moral Principles alluded to by theological and philosophical themes within their own limitations. Candidates are asked to immerse, embrace and dedicate themselves in these portrayed realities. They are also asked to dedicate themselves to these realities and regulate their lives by them.

When you step back and assess with unclouded eyes and heart what is actually going on within the Society of Free & Accepted Masons, you realize very quickly that it is both one theatric production after another and a continuous preparation for the same.

There are plenty of opportunities to learn from participating in both but the only thing that you shall actually receive overtly and purposely from these Freemasonic Productions is a transfer of knowledge that occurs either through preparation or enactment of these plays.

What's more, that transfer of knowledge occurs from the moment you sign the petition and continues all the way through to the highest Degree.

What is Offered

First and foremost, the Society offers members an opportunity to participate in its highly stylized theatrical Performances. This starts with Candidates going through plays called *Degrees.* Progression is regulated by the rules and traditions of each Jurisdiction coupled with the abilities and limits of the Candidate.

Should each Candidate take to heart what is being offered, and take these Degrees beyond simple theater, each can use what was offered to make Better choices in life, both personally and professionally. From that moment on he can apply the codes acted out for his benefit and reap the benefits throughout his life. Should he continue to be a dues paying member, he can continue to come back and review what he initially experienced to assure that he keeps fresh all the rich instruction sets he was offered.

Additional to this, he is offered opportunity to participate in the actual Performances themselves. If he belongs to a Jurisdiction that requires full Proficiencies, he is also prepared to step into any role that is offered him and that he qualifies for within the regulations of the Jurisdiction.

Furthermore, he is entitled to accept the role of specific positions within the Organization itself. These roles are those of *Officers.* Each Officer role requires specific scripts to be followed to assure that it is fully supported. Training is usually offered for these roles at many levels.

Moreover, by virtue of being a member, he is offered opportunity to participate in other Performances, if he qualifies and can afford the fees and time requirements to do so.

Aside from what the Organization offers, the membership also offers many opportunities to bond with others, to contribute and to support auxiliary activities associated with the Society.

Keys to Acting On Purpose

No matter what is offered to you by the Society, there is something far greater that should be considered should you step back and examine the Craft as a whole.

You know that you have found a key to the Mysteries when you realize fully that the Craft is acting at its finest.

You know that you have found another key when you see that the Performance offered by each is not a façade.

You have found yet another key when you recognize that each man is so immersed in his accepted role that he cannot in any way separate himself from the role. *Who each man Is and What each man Does is indistinguishable from each man's Word.*

You see yet another key when you realize that each member authentically portrays himself and who he is, is not untrue in any way.

Perhaps you might come to understand that The Word itself is manifested to the best ability of every societal man you encounter. Realize too that you can be The Word, when you so Desire it that you do the necessary Work to bring it into Being.

XX. The Limelight

When you realize that every Freemasonic Performance is for your Benefit, you might come to Understand the Importance that each should Play in your overall life.

I had occasion shortly before I was to release this book to share its concepts, ideas and information with some few close Brothers and Sisters. Their responses to this Light were universally positive with many responding to me that it all makes perfect sense. Some actually went so far as to say that this view of the origins and practice explains a lot and makes many new connections.

Many went on to say that it fits tongue in grove with what they have observed over the years. It helps explain the huge migration away from coming to meetings and the major attrition. It even helps explain the overall disinterest from inactive members. They realize that they are never going to get from the Society what they were led to believe they would by all the impressive and lofty words that attracted them to the Craft.

Unsettlement

There was one Brother who became disturbingly quiet when I shared this topic with him. I saw him sink into heavy dismay and agitation from what I shared. In his silence, he had come to the conclusion that Freemasonry was one big sham. He said in a soft but firm voice, *"Brother John, tell me there's more to it; that there's light at the end of the tunnel."* I knew what he was asking. I had asked myself this very same question many times after I initially made my connections. I leaned forward, smiled and replied, *"Brother, there's not only Light, but a huge Spotlight"*. And in that statement where I used that one word the light turned on for him and he saw the connection immediately!

The Freemasonic Organization places a Spotlight on every single Candidate going through each of the first three Degrees. Like a limelight in a spectacular production, the Candidate is both highlighted and at the same time shown what role he must play in life to better himself. At each Step along the way he is shown what he must focus upon to Build himself into a Better man.

Apprentice

At first, he is told that he must find himself. That in seeking and doing so, he finds all of humanity. He is told that he must establish what is most important in life. He is shown of what he must divest himself. He is directed toward the time he must spend to reap greater reward. He is asked to build his moral strength. He is encouraged to establish and maintain boundaries and to never exceed them for any ungodly reason.

He is furthermore given an enormous opportunity to commit to all this with a clear and unwavering understanding that he shall suffer personally and by his own hand for not adhering to his intended course of action. Men, who take this Degree to heart, cultivate exactly that. They establish Order within it. And by doing so, they also gain tremendous insight in their fellow man and bring under rule their animal nature. This is just at the first level!

Fellow Craft

In the second Degree, Candidates are provided more opportunity to commit to Betterment. They are shown what must be learned to learn! They are given examples of what it take to learn how to distinguish and differentiate even the most subtle things that others with untrained minds would leave unnoticed. They are also provided the *Staircase to Heaven,* in that should they take the necessary steps to cultivate their minds, bringing order to chaos within their very thoughts. When done, they shall establish a strong foundation of mind to explore their Faith as only a true scholar can.

Each Candidate is again given another enormous opportunity to commit to all this with a clear and unwavering understanding that he shall self-inflict personal suffering for not adhering to his intended course of action.

Master

At the third and final Blue Lodge Degree, Candidates are provided further opportunities to commit to furthering their personal development and cultivating themselves. They are also encouraged to explore the universe of meta-meaning. They are individually *carried through a Tragedy* by their more experienced Brothers and offered the chance to test their ability to strip the many veils away from their experience. If they have done the Work of the previous Degrees, they shall realize the drama has multiple levels of meaning and is a test of their abilities to not be fooled into thinking any of what occurred was factual or historical. Yet, the truths conveyed are life changing, when they are recognized, understood and applied toward the Candidates life!

He is once again given an enormous opportunity to commit to all this with a clear and unwavering understanding that he shall suffer personally and by his own hand for not adhering to his intended course of action.

XXI. Curtain Call

When you accurately describe the land you wish
to Travel, you are better able to navigate
within it, through it or around it.

For some time now I have described Freemasonic Ritual as *"Roadmaps for Personal Transformation"*. Describing Ritual in this way has enabled me and quite a few other Brothers to delve into what they point toward. This view better enabled us to use these Maps for the ends to which we entered the Society. Perhaps it's time to describe Freemasonry as a whole so that members overall shall be enabled to both Better themselves and the organization. Let's start with future members.

From the view of incoming Candidates, the operation of the Fraternity is that which is assumed to be styled after Medieval Stoneworkers guilds, especially when it comes to what is conveyed as the hierarchy of the Organization at the Lodge level. They are led to believe that this is how the Stoneworkers' Lodges were set up and how they did their business. The Lexicon is present throughout the Lodge as both verbal and symbolic cues, especially while at Labor. They are from the very beginning immersed in a World that is foreign to them and filled with mystery and confusion.

With time comes clarity, but it is a clarity wrought towards the reality of the play put before them and without an anchor, they are swept away by the Performance. If they are like the majority, they too shall never make the leap to comprehend fully the truth that is being offered them through allusion.

The Future

So little is shared with Candidates about what they truly should expect beyond experiencing the Degree Performances and perhaps doing rudimentary Proficiencies.

This is a statement that I share with Brothers who have just gone through any one of the Symbolic Lodge Degrees. Feel free to share it as you want and as you can:

Congratulations my Brother. What you have just experienced is a Road Map of Masonic Progression provided to you by your loving Brothers. It is one of Three Road Maps that you experience within the Symbolic Lodge Educational system. Each Road Map provides you a direction to make yourself a Better man.

Your Brothers shall Coach and Mentor you toward becoming Proficient in remembering each of these Road maps. They shall also help you to install them within your head and hopefully within your heart.

I caution you earnestly though to remember always that the work you do installing each Map is not the Work that makes you a Better man. That Work is performed by you when you take each map out, Recognize it for what it is, Understand the Work toward which it points you and then Applying it by Travelling the Territory it represents and do the Work.

Keep in mind always that no Map is a Territory. Should you merely memorize these Maps without following them, you shall be no Better off than had you not bothered to memorize them at all. Should you want to be a Better man, you must do the Work that each Degree directs you toward. Your Brothers should know this well and you can hopefully rely upon them to assist you in doing just that. If they can't, find ones who can.

152

Once you have Traveled these Territories, Learned well their varying Terrains, and Established the Strengths that each are intended to bring forth within you, your Word shall open up your world in ways you cannot begin to imagine.

A final word of caution, Maps are not Substitutes for the real thing. Should you merely memorize these Maps, accept them as real and Travel not the Territories they direct you toward, you shall bar yourself from the world they are supposed to offer you.

Once again, I congratulate you and wish you well in all your Travels.

– Brother John S Nagy

Afterthought

It is utterly amazing the questions and comments that come forth once you place a Spotlight upon what you engage.

This could be considered another chapter of this book, but in truth it really isn't. I write it now as an Afterthought spurred on by some of the comments and questions shared with me by the reviewers and editors of this book. As their comments and question came in, I took the time to explore each one to see how they might add to the value of this book. I made a conscious decision to place them here at the end. Why? Well, read on and perhaps you may be able to answer this for yourself.

I: Are there any other goat connections?

R: Yes. The connection is that of a scapegoat. Whether it involved a preacher, a dictator or a conspiracy monger, each found tremendous leverage using Freemasonry as a scapegoat for their serious folly. For centuries, Freemasonic themes, principles and

organizations have been pointed toward by them, blamed for the ills of the societies and cultures surrounding them and used as a rallying point to gain advantage over others.

I: **How many men died or were imprisoned over a play?**

R: This question was raised without respect to the sensitivities of those members, including myself, who consider Freemasonry more than mere plays. But the question was put forth none the less with earnest sincerity and due interest. The question got my interest immediately and I was soon directed toward *"Suppression of Freemasonry",* an article posted on Wikipedia. As I read through it, I was startled when I read the following:

The number of Freemasons from Nazi occupied countries who were killed is not accurately known, but it is estimated that between 80,000 and 200,000 Freemasons were murdered under the Nazi regime. [65]

This information was based upon only one of many wars and one of many dictatorships that came into power over the past three hundred years. Considering how many wars and tyrannies occurred since its Grand Lodge beginning, you can only imagine how many other members were killed or imprisoned.

I: **Was all this really just over a dangerous play?**

R: No. It was over what the entire Society represented to these dictators and tyrants. Men promised in these Society plays to be moral no matter what and they meant it. Promises like this were threatening to men who want citizen control no matter what it cost.

I: **Why was the Premier Grand Lodge formed?**

R: This was an interesting question to research and I confess that I have not done so extensively. From the few sites and books that I have read on the subject, they appear to all confirm that the reason was fairly simple. The Premier Grand Lodge was formed around 1717 CE to engage in quarterly dinner parties.[66] Eating, drinking, toasting and singing were an integral part of the gatherings with many songs appearing in its Constitutions. This is in stark contrast to the sterile business meetings occurring today. I add to this that these latter meetings are dedicated to preserving Ritual that clearly didn't exist at the time of the first Grand Lodge gathering.

I: **Was there something that you discovered while writing this book that made you giggle?**

R: Yes. My book writing efforts are fun filled adventures for me and this one was no different. The connection of the Craft to Mystery plays was a delight. The connection between the Greek letter Theta and the Circumpunct was as well. The reason the Premier Grand Lodge was formed presented a good laugh. Each and every connection with the goat brought forth a lot of smiles too. I think though that the one thing that caused me to both scratch my head in wonder and then laugh out loud was a simple sketched curtain illustration. I came across two of them while I was looking for illustrations for this book. The first one was open and you can see it at the beginning of this *Afterthought.* It is a standard configuration that shows the curtains pulled back by two draw strings attached to the center where the two curtains meet.

The second illustration is shown at the end of this *Afterthought.* It shows the two curtains undrawn and relaxed. When I looked at this second picture I was jolted. At first I thought that I had somehow stumbled upon a Freemasonic site. The illustrated curtain draw strings looked just like the flap and apron strings on a Masonic Apron! When I finally realized that I had mistaken the curtain for an apron, I couldn't stop laughing.

I found it to be too much of an ironic coincidence to not use the illustration in this book.

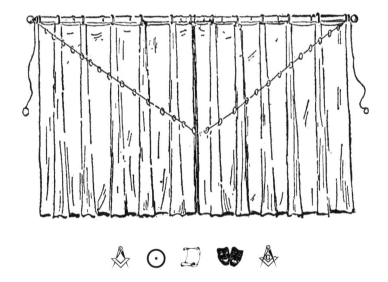

Appendices

A. <u>Rough Time Line of Craft Practice</u>

Century	Event(s)
6th Century BCE	Craft Practice is conceived by Innovation; The first man steps forth and Practices the Craft.
5th Century CE	Fall of the Roman Empire; Craft Practice is condemned by the Church.
10th Century CE	Craft Practice is adopted by the Church.
13th Century CE	The Church distances itself from public Craft Practice; Many guilds adopt Public Craft Practice.
16th Century CE	Professionals take over; Most guilds stop public Craft Practice as too costly
17th Century CE	Stonecraft guilds begin Accepting members as Craft Patrons and Practitioners
18th Century CE	Freemasonic Premier Grand Lodge is formed; Craft Practices are standardized, privatized and franchised; Other Grand Lodges form using similar materials; Propaganda about Craft origins and Practice multiplies; Higher Degrees are created and standardized
21th Century CE	Craft Practice and its actual origin are identified

B. <u>About the Author</u>

As of this writing, Brother John S. Nagy is a Master Mason, Lodge Musician, and 2014 recipient of the Duane E. Anderson Award for Excellence in Masonic Education. He provides Masonic Education to his Lodges and for others who support his efforts to share.

John is also author of the *"Building Better Builders Series"* of Uncommon Masonic Education books. His books: *Building Hiram, Building Boaz, Building Athens, Building Janus, Building Perpends, Building Ruffish, Building Cement*, and *Building Free Men*, his videos: *"The Coaches Coach: Building Builders"* Parts 1 & 2 and *Masonic Cement* and his *Uncommon Masonic Education Workshops* cover aspects of Masonry designed to Build Better Builders.

Coach Nagy's materials are used to instruct Blue Lodge, Scottish Rite and York Rite Candidates in *Symbol Recognition, Understanding and Application.*

Professionally, Coach Nagy is a multi degree Professional Business Coach and Technical Advisor who provides coaching support to business professionals through his home office in Florida. He has been in the coaching field since January 1989, running his own coaching practice.

John is also a Florida State Certified County Mediator who mediates county level cases to assist in lessening the burden upon the local courts. He has been actively engaged in Mediation work since 1995.

You can find out more about John, his books, his videos and his workshops through his website page found at: http://www.coach.net

C. <u>Points to Perpend</u>

Chapter I.

1) How many times have shared Light and found Brothers resistant to its slightest hints?
2) Where do you find Brothers who are more open to hearing your thoughts?
3) What do you think about the Assumption that many men make as to the Origins of the Craft?

Chapter II.

1) What misunderstandings have you experienced that were fueled by differences in word meaning?
2) How do you convey your understanding while remaining open to how your words were being understood by others?
3) How successful are you in exchanging ideas and thoughts without getting bogged by meanings?

Chapter III.

1) What further differences do you see between Stonecraft and Freemasonry?
2) What do you imagine the True Craft that is being Practiced by Freemasons?
3) How did you come to this Conclusion?

Chapter IV.

1) How much of what you have been told about the Craft differs from what you actually see?
2) How does this contrast affect your enthusiasm for the Organization?
3) How would you go about characterizing the Craft?

Chapter V.

1) How do you hear the word *Mysteries* being used within Freemasonic Ritual?
2) Do you take the word to mean *Secrets* or *Work* or *both?*
3) What do you imagine to be the connection between *Mystery Plays* and *Freemasonry?*

Chapter VI.

1) How would you go about exploring the evolution of Vernacular plays during the middle ages?
2) What connections do you see between the Impresario and any of the current Freemasonic Lodge officers?
3) Which officer would you say best relates to the Impresario of the guilds?

Chapter VIII.

1) What do you think that you are doing as a member of the Freemasonic Society?
2) Have you thought that you were doing anything other than well-scripted plays?
3) What are your thoughts as to what the originators of these plays were making effort to accomplish?

Chapter VIII.

1) What impact do you believe Freemasonic Plays have upon those who participate in them?
2) When taken at face value, whom do you have to Be

to put your Freemasonic activities into proper prospective?
3) How can you use the Light of this writing to better participate in your Freemasonic Activities?

Chapter IX.

1) What moral lessons have you been taught directly by the Society that helped you become a Better man as a result?
2) What training have you received through the Society that supported your becoming a Better man?
3) Do you know exactly what Society Ritual points toward that if pursued would continue to help transform you toward the Better?

Chapter X.

1) What difference do you think it would make for Candidates to familiarize themselves with the meanings behind what they are to experience?
2) If you were to experience an Initiation Rite, would

you want to know more about the significance of the experience and what it uses to convey that significance before or after the fact?

3) If you were to step upon sacred ground, would it mean more to you knowing this fact before you stepped upon it or long after you left that soil?

Chapter XI.

1) What do you think the Craft is that you have been trained to employ.

2) Who have you thought yourself to be as you were learning the Craft?

3) What difference would it have made to you if you were told upfront in what you were actually asked to engage?

Chapter XII.

1) What skill development support were you offered by your Lodge?

2) Was it memorization or was it in line with what the Degrees espoused?

3) How do you feel about what was offered in relation to what was espoused?

Chapter XIII.

1) How many similarities do you see in what was shared in this chapter and the Lore and practice of Freemasonry?

2) What do you think about the Society's connection with the goat as you were reading about Tragic word roots?

3) How much Dramatization of Freemasonry do you see in your Brother's behaviors as it is being acted out inside and outside the Lodge?

Chapter XIV.

1) How well did the Society Properly Prepare you to Play a Part within its Degree plays?

2) What impact upon your life did playing these roles have upon you?

3) Could the Society have done any more to properly prepare?

162

Chapter XV.

1) What did you imagine about the Craft prior to Joining?
2) What did you discover about it once you joined?
3) What possible conspiracy do you think is acted out by the Society?

Chapter XVI.

1) How would you describe the many layers of the organization and its Practiced Craft?
2) How do you see yourself using this Light into your Future?
3) What difference do you imagine this Light to make for yourself and those you support?

Chapter XVII.

1) How true have you been able to portray the Character you claim to be worthwhile emulating?
2) What have you accurately portray so far?
3) What must you do differently to portray a more authentic Performance?

Chapter XVIII.

1) What have you thought The Word to be?
2) How have you thoughts changed over the years?
3) What do you think The Word is currently?

Chapter XIX.

1) What did you believe the Society offered to you when you first joined?
2) Did it offer what you expected?
3) What can you explain Better for others who are interested in joining so that their expectations are more realistic or at least more reasonable?

Chapter XX.

1) What insights into your person did you receive as a result of experiencing the three Degree Performances'?
2) How did you choice change as a result of these insights'?
3) What has improved in your life as a result of these choice changes?

D. Cipher Key

```
⌐ ⌐ ⊔ ⨆ ∟ ∟ ⊐ ⊐ ◻ ◻ ⊏ ⊏ ⌐ ⌐ ⊓ ⊓ ⌐ ⌐ ∨ ∨ > > < < ∧ ∧
A B C D E F G H I J K L M N O P Q R S T U V W X Y Z
```

```
⌐ ⌐ ⊔ ⨆ ∟ ∟ ⊐ ⊐ ◻ ◻ ⊏ ⊏ ⌐ ⌐ ⊓ ⊓ ⌐ ⌐ ∨ ∨ > > < < ∧ ∧
A B C D E F G H I J K L M N O P Q R S T U V W X Y Z
```

```
⌐ ⌐ ⊔ ⨆ ∟ ∟ ⊐ ⊐ ◻ ◻      ⌐ ⌐ ⊔ ⨆ ∟ ∟ ⊐ ⊐ ◻ ◻
1 2 3 4 5 6 7 8 9 0      1 2 3 4 5 6 7 8 9 0
```

E. Mysteries and Pageants in England

(This article was originally published in <u>A Short History of the Drama</u>. Martha Fletcher Bellinger. New York: Henry Holt and Company, 1927. pp. 132-7. Although the entire article is interesting, the underlined sections are of significance to this book and its themes.)

It is probable that the sacred play was brought to England from France after the Norman conquest. Throughout the fourteenth, fifteenth, and sixteenth centuries there was a constant supply of mysteries and miracles. More than one hundred English towns, some of them very small, are known to have been provided with these entertainments, which in some places were given every year. Usually, however, an interval of a few years elapsed between productions. Corpus Christi day, which falls in early June, was the most popular time, though Whitsuntide and occasionally other Church festal days were marked by performances. On one occasion the Parish Clerks gave a pageant which lasted for three days, and again one lasting for eight days. The boy choristers of Saint

Paul's in London became celebrated for their histrionic ability, and in 1378 they begged Parliament to issue an injunction against "unskilled performers." In 1416 Henry V entertained the Emperor Sigismund at Windsor with a play on the subject of Saint George; and in the following year the English bishops who were delegated to the Council of Constance--the same Council which promised safe conduct to John Huss and then burned him at the stake--entertained their hosts with a Christmas play in three parts, the *Nativity,* the *Visit of the Magi,* and the *Slaughter of the Innocents.* Two performances were given, one for their fellow councillors and themselves, the other for the burghers of the town.

Some of the extant manuscripts. The usual name for these plays in England was *miracle,* or the Latin *ludus,* or sometimes the word *history.* The name *mystery* is said to have been first applied, in England, in the early eighteenth century by Dodsley, the editor of a volume of old plays. Of the extant manuscripts, the earliest is probably the *Harrowing of Hell,* in three versions, all of which were probably taken from the French. It is simply a dramatic dialogue in verse, in which Christ and Satan argue over the ownership of the souls in hell; and it belongs naturally with the Easter group of plays. Two plays were discovered during the twentieth century, one on the subject of *Abraham and Isaac;* the other, belonging to the lost Newcastle Cycle, on the *Building of the Ark,* both probably surviving from the fourteenth century.

The Cycles. The greater part of the important manuscripts of biblical drama belongs to the cycles--a medieval product in a sense peculiar to England--which attempted to cover the history of Man from his creation to the Day of Judgment. In these cycles there appeared, almost unconsciously, something like the principle of unity: first came the creation, then the fall of Man, which necessitated his redemption. This redemption, after being foretold by the prophets, was accomplished by the birth and passion of Christ, with his resurrection. The series, taken as a whole, formed a true dramatic sequence, in which the soul of Man was the hero.

There are commonly counted four important English cycles: Chester, York, Coventry, and Towneley (also called Wakefield). Cycles are also known to have been produced at Newcastle, Canterbury, and Lincoln. Of those that survive, the Chester cycle is probably the earliest. Of the Newcastle cycle but one play remains, *The Building of the Ark*, in which there are five characters, and Noah's wife is represented as a vixen. Such is her stubborn temper that Noah is constrained to say to her,

> "The devil of hell thee speed
> To ship when thou shalt go!"

The cycles vary in quality, and the plays are not always the work of one hand, nor even of one century. The manuscripts, as we have them, have been revised, edited, and arranged, probably from several earlier models, possibly in some cases from the French. In the different cycles there is naturally great similarity both in subject matter and in the sequence of plays; but there are also interesting differences of treatment.

The Pageant. Doubtless biblical plays were often given in England in the continental manner, on a stationary platform with the "mansions" arranged in proper order. Gradually, however, the pageant became specially associated with the English play. The word first meant the movable scaffolding upon which the play was given, but was afterward applied to the play itself. Reduced to its simplest elements, the pageant was a play on wheels. This of course was not a new thing. Tradition assigns a cart to Thespis; there were "carriage plays" in Spain; and traveling shows in Japan. In England, as a rule, each play of the cycle had its own carriage, and all moved along in procession, each wagon giving its play in turn at each stopping place. Usually the pageant began very early in the morning. In the proclamation of the York performances in 1415, it was announced that the plays would begin between four and five o'clock in the morning.

All our knowledge concerning the method of presenting the pageant comes from a report left by one Archdeacon Rogers, who wrote of it in quaint English about the year 1517. He said that each carriage had a higher and a lower room, the lower "where they appareled themselves," and the higher where they played. Temporary stands were built for spectators, and good seats sold for high prices. Sometimes the action of the play called for horsemen, in which case obviously the action would spread out beyond the limits of the stage. The celebration opened with a procession, and after its close there was an orderly round-up by the councilmen and mayor. One writer says:

"To a medieval town the performance of a mystery was an event of immense interest. . . . the magistrates ordered all the shops to be closed, and forbade all noisy work. The streets were empty, the houses locked up, and none but solitary armed watch-men, specially engaged for the occasion, were seen about the residences. All were gathered in the public square." [Karl Mantzius, *History of the Theatrical Art.*]

The Guilds. We have seen how in France the production of plays, once having left the hands of the clergy, passed into the care of certain Brotherhoods. In England the production was managed by the tradesmen's guilds. Each play was arranged, acted, costumed, and financed by its own guild. A study of the distribution of the plays among the guilds forms one of the diverting features of this medieval carnival. In the York cycle the tinners began with *God Creating Heaven*; the plasterers followed with *God Creating the Earth*; and then came the cardmakers, with *God Creating Man*. Of course, the shipbuilders and seamen played *Noah and the Ark*, while the goldsmiths enacted the *Three Kings*, because they could furnish gold crowns. The guilds took pride in making a good showing, being inspired doubtless by both the spirit of good workmanship and the desire to advertise their wares. The smiths had the task of affixing the body of Christ to the cross. A dialogue between the torturers in one of the Towneley plays indicates how one holds down the limbs with all his might. They then congratulated themselves that neither "lewde man ne clerke nothing better shuld."

Scenery, costumes, and finance. In the larger towns considerable time and care were spent in preparation for the pageants. The scenery and stage appliances must have been somewhat scant, if all were accommodated in a rolling greenroom and stage combined. The splendor of the costumes perhaps made up for anything that was lacking in the setting. It was the custom for God to wear a white coat and have his face gilded. Herod, and miscreants generally, were dressed in Saracens, they being the stage villains of the Middle Ages. The expenses, which were often large, were sometimes partly met by a nobleman or other public spirited benefactor; but in general the citizens or guilds financed the production. A collection was taken up at the time of the procession; and, in addition, a tax, ranging from a penny to fourpence and called pageant silver, was imposed upon each member of the guilds. It was paid over to the pageant master, who was elected each year. Today he would be called the business manager, or impresario. The actors and "drawers" were paid for their services; but there was a fine for bad acting or undue forgetfulness of the parts, also fines for guilds which were slow in handing over their pageant silver.

The most impressive of all the mysteries was the *Passion of Christ*; and this was, as we have seen, also the earliest to be dramatized. In England it took shape about the fourteenth century, gradually showing the conflict between the spiritual strength of Jesus, on the one hand, and on the other the combined forces of the Jewish and Roman worlds. Of all the ecclesiastical plays, this alone can still be seen enacted in modern times.

Lack of artistic quality in biblical plays. Theoretically, the escape of the liturgical plays from the control of the Church, the extension of subjects and the possibility of greater freedom of treatment, ought to have enabled the dramatists to produce at least one masterpiece; but none such exists. Here and there are passages of such sturdy simplicity, so sincere and pleasing, that they for a moment seem to lift the play out of a dull and commonplace atmosphere into one of life and reality; but there is not one genius of the first rank, not one play of the quality of *Macbeth* or *Oedipus* in all the enormous output of the Middle Ages. One mystery is just about as good, and just about as dull, as another. So poor did the plays become that a celebrated French writer, Du Bellay, publicly advocated the importation of Greek and Roman tragedy to take the place of the native mysteries. There was none of that struggling with the problems of life and destiny which marks the tragedy of the Greeks; no attainment of an artificial but beautiful conventional form, such as appeared in the *No* plays of the Japanese; only an occasional naïve touch, interesting because of its spontaneous simplicity.

The decline and disappearance of the biblical play. The next phase of the sacred play is just what might be expected, namely, its condemnation by the Church under whose protection it had risen. It was condemned, however, not only by the Church. The time came when the hollowness, the absence of all religious feeling, made the performance a disgrace and a scandal. A pious habit had become a conventionalized and empty show. Both Romanists and Protestants ultimately frowned upon the mysteries, and denounced them for their childishness and coarseness. The guilds, which had once gladly given time and money for their preparation, now felt the yearly tax a burden. The cycle of sacred drama had run its course. In France, performances were forbidden during the latter part of the sixteenth century. In Spain and in Catholic Germany, as well as in Italy, they persisted somewhat longer. In England they were forbidden by Henry VIII, but were restored again for a brief time under Mary. There were few performances after 1600. The last York play was in 1597, the last Newcastle play in 1589. The Chester plays died out with the sixteenth century. The most important result of all this dramatic activity was perhaps the fostering of a love for the theater, and the shaping of native material into rough dramatic form.

F. Decline of Religious Drama

(This document was originally published in The Drama: Its History, Literature and Influence on Civilization, vol. 7. ed. Alfred Bates. London: Historical Publishing Company, 1906. pp. 11-13. Although the entire article is interesting, the underlined sections are of significance to this book and its themes.)

Notwithstanding the intermittent hostility of the Parlement [sic], farce outlived the graver drama from which it sprang. For some time past the popularity of the Mysteries and Miracles had been steadily declining. They had been spun out until the representation of the shortest occupied days, and the most pious spectator must have found them wearisome. They had ceased to be in harmony with the temper of the age. The dawn of latter-day civilization had broadened into what seemed almost as the perfect day. The intellectual agitation induced by the events of the last hundred years--the revival of ancient literature, the overthrow of the Ptolemaic system, the downfall of the Moors in Spain, the discoveries of Iberian navigators, political changes and the partial liberation of the Church-- had lifted the human mind out of the narrow ruts in which it had so long been content to move. New ideas began to hold sway; an ardent and restless spirit of inquiry was abroad in the land; opinions which seemed to be bound up with life itself were rejected or essentially altered. Unlike other medieval institutions, chivalry not excepted, religion emerged with added strength from the ordeal; for while a vague skepticism may have found expression in the pages of Rabelais and Montaigne, among the nation at large the old child-like simplicity of faith gave way to a higher sense of the dignity and grandeur of Christianity.

The Renaissance also served to raise the standard of literary taste, inasmuch as, aided by the invention of printing, it was bringing imperishable monuments of ancient poetry and prose within the reach of all who could read. Under these circumstances the sacred drama, with its odd intermixture of the sublime and the grotesque, its crudeness of form and substance, rapidly lost the charm it had once possessed. Catholics and Huguenots united in denouncing it as likely to bring religion into contempt, and its defects in the way of style were glaring enough to evoke a flood of ridicule. The Brethren of the Passion, so far from appreciating the necessity of reforming their entertainments, sought to compensate themselves for the coldness of the lettered playgoers by appealing more than ever to the unlettered--in other words, by giving increased prominence to satire and scandal. By this change of policy they simply accelerated their doom; and a few years later, the French religious drama, the oldest institution of the kind in western Europe, passed away with the state of society which permitted such things to exist.

Condemnation of Secular Drama

The great majority of the priesthood could not reconcile themselves to the purely secular drama, especially after they saw that a great revolution was in progress about them. Might not the theatre be employed to disseminate ideas more or less inimical to their doctrines and pretensions? Were they not really warming a viper in their bosom? The decree of 1548, abolishing the religious drama, did away with the only reason they had for dissembling their hostility to the farce--namely, a reluctance to throw discredit upon an institution which partly devoted itself to the service of Christianity. Henceforward the clergy were uncompromising opponents of theatrical amusement in any shape. They reprehended play-going as incompatible with true devotion, purity of life and sobriety of thought. They condemned the actor to a kind of social outlawry, declaring that, unless he solemnly forswore his profession, he could not receive the holy communion or be entitled to Christian burial.

G. Recommended Readings

1) **Building Hiram**   – Volume 1
2) **Building Boaz**   – Volume 2
3) **Building Athens**   – Volume 3
4) **Building Janus**   – Volume 4

5) **Building Perpends** – Volume 5
6) **Building Ruffish** – Volume 6
7) **Building Cement** – Volume 7
8) **Building Free Men** – Volume 8
9) Emotional Awareness **Made Easy**
10) **Provoking Success**
11) **The Power of Myth** – Joseph Campbell
12) **Holy Scriptures** (**Gnostic Gospels** included!)
13) **Dictionaries** (with word roots and histories)

H. <u>End Notes</u>

---

[1] **FREEMASONS**, n. An order with secret rites, grotesque
ceremonies and fantastic costumes, which, originating in the
reign of Charles II, among working artisans of London, has
been joined successively by the dead of past centuries in
unbroken retrogression until now it embraces all the
generations of man on the hither side of Adam and is
drumming up distinguished recruits among the pre-Creational
inhabitants of Chaos and Formless Void. The order was
founded at different times by Charlemagne, Julius Caesar,
Cyrus, Solomon, Zoroaster, Confucius, Thothmes, and Buddha.
Its emblems and symbols have been found in the Catacombs
of Paris and Rome, on the stones of the Parthenon and the
Chinese Great Wall, among the temples of Karnak and Palmyra
and in the Egyptian Pyramids -- always by a Freemason. The
Devil's Dictionary; Ambrose Bierce. The World Publishing
Company: Cleveland and New York. 1941. p. 108.
http://freemasonry.bcy.ca/biography/bierce_a/bierce_freemas
onry.html

[2] **Bro. Albert Mackey's Encyclopedia of Freemasonry**, 1917
edition pages 333-335

[3] Some Offered Working Definitions

[4] A Promulgated Script, kept hidden from the view of members
and non-members, except for specific occasions where the pages
may be viewed for a limited time with approval from the Grand

Lodge by members and hinted at through ciphers and codes.

[5] (adjective) 1. strange or odd; unusual. 2. belonging exclusively to. (noun) [British] 1. a parish or church exempt from the jurisdiction of the diocese in which it lies, through being subject to the jurisdiction of the monarch or an archbishop. [Origin] late Middle English (in the sense 'particular, special'): from Latin *peculiaris* 'of private property,' from *peculium* 'property,' from pecu 'cattle' (cattle being private property). The sense 'odd' dates from the early 17th century.

[6] 1. principles concerning the distinction between right and wrong or good and bad behavior. 2. virtue, goodness, good behavior, righteousness, rectitude, uprightness; principles, morals, honesty, integrity, propriety, honor, justice, decency; ethics, standards and principles of behavior, mores, standards 3. particular system of values and principles of conduct, especially one held by a specified person or society. 4. the extent to which an action is determined to be right or wrong. 5. [archaic] plays intended and designed to convey mores.

[7] [Origin] late 16th century (in the sense 'dignified, aloof'): from Latin *sublimis,* from sub- 'up to' + a second element perhaps related to *limen* 'threshold,' *limus* 'oblique.'

[8] [Origin: Australian/New Zealand] mid 19th century (referring to mining): probably from the English dialect sense "obtain by asking" (i.e., 'ferret out').

[9] [Synonyms] dissimulation, false virtue, cant, posturing, affectation, speciousness, empty talk, insincerity, falseness, deceit, dishonesty, mendacity, pretense, duplicity; sanctimony, pietism, piousness, sanctimoniousness, phoniness, [Antonym] sincerity [Origin] Middle English: c.1200, ipocrisie, from Old French ypocrisie, from Late Latin hypocrisis, from Greek hypokrisis "acting on the stage, pretense," from hypokrinesthai "play a part, pretend," also "answer," from hypo- "under" (see sub-) + middle voice of krinein "to sift, decide, judge". The sense evolution in Attic Greek is from "separate gradually" to "answer" to "answer a fellow actor on stage" to "*play a part.*" *The h- was restored in English 16c.*

[10] Tweaked from : Shakespeare, As You Like It, Act II, Scene VII

[11] Building Free Men – Uncommonly Freeing Masonic Education - Volume 8; Dr. John S. Nagy

---

[12] Seek first to understand, then to be understood – Habit #5; Seven Habits of Highly Effective People; Stephen Covey

[13] Building Free Men – Uncommonly Freeing Masonic Education; Dr. John S. Nagy (2014)

[14] Stonemasonry – Wikipedia

[15] Ibid

[16] Ibid

[17] Ibid

[18] Ibid

[19] Ibid

[20] Ibid

[21] Acceptable Admittance (Chapter IV – Building Free Men – Uncommonly Freeing Masonic Education – Volume 8)

[22] Non-members of the Society

[23] **Time Immemorial** is a phrase meaning time extending beyond the reach of memory, record, or tradition, indefinitely ancient, "ancient beyond memory or record".[Oxford English Dictionary (1971 ed.), Vol. I, p. 63c] The phrase is one of the few cases in the English language where the adjective is a postmodifier—some other phrases, such as the legal terms attorney general and court-martial, also follow that pattern, largely due to the influence of Norman French.

In law, it means that a property or benefit has been enjoyed for so long that its owner does not have to prove how they came to own it. The term has been formally defined for some purposes:

In English law and its derivatives, time immemorial means the same as time out of mind,[Blackstone (1765) *Commentary* I viii 281] "a time before legal history and beyond legal memory."[The public domain Webster's Revised Unabridged Dictionary (1913)] In 1275, by the first Statute of Westminster, the time of memory was limited to the reign of Richard I (Richard the Lionheart), beginning 6 July 1189, the date of the King's accession.[Statute of Westminster, The First (3 Edw. I cap. 5)] Since that date, proof of unbroken possession or use of any right made it unnecessary to establish the original grant under certain circumstances. In 1832, time immemorial was re-defined as "Time whereof the Memory of Man runneth not to the contrary."[Prescription Act,

The (2 & 3 Will. IV cap. /1) s.1] The plan of dating legal memory from a fixed time was abandoned; instead, it was held that rights which had been enjoyed for twenty years (or as against the Crown thirty years) should not be impeached merely by proving that they had not been enjoyed before (holding by adverse possession).

The High Court of Chivalry is said to have defined the period before 1066 as time immemorial for the purposes of heraldry. [About the College of Arms College of Arms (retrieved 24 May 2010)] Source:
http://en.wikipedia.org/wiki/Time_immemorial

[24] Of Old English origin, and the meaning of Athelstan is "noble stone".

[25] **mystery** (n.1) *"handicraft, trade, art"* (archaic), late 14c., from Medieval Latin *misterium*, alteration of Latin *ministerium* *"service, occupation, office, ministry"* (influenced in form by Medieval Latin *mysterium* (*see mystery (n.2)*) and in sense by *maistrie* "mastery see ministry)."

mystery (n.2) early 14c., in a theological sense, *"religious truth via divine revelation, hidden spiritual significance, mystical truth,"* from Anglo-French *misterie, Old French mistere "secret, mystery, hidden meaning"* (Modern French mystère), from Latin *mysterium "secret rite, secret worship; a secret thing,"* from Greek *mysterion* (usually in plural *mysteria*) *"secret rite or doctrine,"* from *mystes "one who has been initiated,"* from *myein "to close, shut"*)); perhaps referring to the lips (in secrecy) or to the eyes *(only initiates were allowed to see the sacred rites).*

The Greek word was used in Septuagint for *"secret counsel of God,"* translated in Vulgate as *sacramentum.* Non-theological use in English, *"a hidden or secret thing,"* is from late 14c. In reference to the ancient rites of Greece, Egypt, etc. it is attested from 1640s.

The two senses of *mystery* formed a common pun in (secular) Tudor theater.

[26] **Mystery**; page 300; *The Concise Dictionary of English Etymology;* Walter W. Skeat

[27] http://www.etymonline.com/index.php?term=mystery; (2001-2014); (2001-2014) Douglas Harper

[28] **Miracle play**, also called **Saint's Play**, one of three principal kinds of vernacular drama of the European Middle Ages (along with the mystery play and the morality play). A miracle play presents a real or fictitious account of the life, miracles, or martyrdom of a saint. The genre evolved from liturgical offices developed during the 10th and 11th centuries to enhance calendar festivals. By the 13th century they had become vernacularized and filled with unecclesiastical elements. They had been divorced from church services and were performed at public festivals. Almost all surviving miracle plays concern either the Virgin Mary or St. Nicholas, the 4th-century bishop of Myra in Asia Minor. Both Mary and Nicholas had active cults during the Middle Ages, and belief in the healing powers of saintly relics was widespread. In this climate, miracle plays flourished. (Encyclopedia Britannica)

[29] **Trope** (literature) [From Wikipedia] "A literary trope is the use of figurative language – via word, phrase, or even an image – for artistic effect such as using a figure of speech. The word trope has also come to be used for describing commonly recurring literary and rhetorical devices, motifs or clichés in creative works. The term trope derives from the Greek τρόπος (tropos), 'turn, direction, way', derived from the verb τρέπειν (trepein), 'to turn, to direct, to alter, to change'. Tropes and their classification were an important field in classical rhetoric. The study of tropes has been taken up again in modern criticism, especially in deconstruction. Tropological criticism is the historical study of tropes, which aims to 'define the dominant tropes of an epoch' and to 'find those tropes in literary and non-literary texts', an interdisciplinary investigation of whom Michel Foucault was an 'important exemplar'.

A specialized use is the medieval amplification of texts from the liturgy, such as in the Kyrie Eleison (Kyrie, / magnae Deus potentia, / liberator hominis, / transgressoris mandati, / eleison). The most important example of such a trope is the Quem quaeritis?, an amplification before the Introit of the Easter Sunday service and the source for liturgical drama. This particular practice came to an end with the Tridentine Mass, the unification of the liturgy in 1570 promulgated by Pope Pius V."

[30] 1210 CE

[31] ...from which the former had relied heavily upon from the latter for their source materials.

[32] **Impresario** (noun) – 1. a person who organizes and often finances concerts, plays, or operas. [synonyms] organizer, (stage) manager, producer; promoter, publicist, showman. 2. director, conductor, maestro

3. [Historical] the manager of a musical, theatrical, or operatic company. [Origin] mid 18th century: from Italian, from *impresa* "**undertaking**".

[33] Martha Fletcher Bellinger

[34] A Short History of the Drama. Martha Fletcher Bellinger. New York: Henry Holt and Company, 1927. pp. 132-7.)

[35] *The Letter G* by Bro. Mark Dwor; (This paper is based on an article written by Harry Carr, P.A.G.D.C., P.M., Secretary of the Quatuor Coronati Lodge, 1963, in Volume 76 of the Transaction of that Lodge, page 170.)

[36] The Hiramic Legend: Whence & Wherefore by W:. Bro. Chakravarthy Sampath Madhavan; http://www.freemasons-freemasonry.com/MADHAVAN_HiramicLegend.html

[37] The Rituals of American Freemasonry by W:. Bro. Ron Blaisdell; June 16, 2001; http://www.themasonictrowel.com/ebooks/fm_freemasonry/Blaisdell_-_The_Rituals_of_American_Freemasonry.pdf

[38] http://www.molor.org/trumanlectureseries#spring2012

[39] Freemasonry in Black and White; Charles M. Harper Sr. (2013)

[40] Oxford English Dictionary (1971 ed.), Vol. I, p. 63c

[41] Blackstone (1765) Commentary I viii 281

[42] The public domain Webster's Revised Unabridged Dictionary (1913)

[43] Statute of Westminster, The First (3 Edw. I cap. 5)

[44] Prescription Act, The (2 & 3 Will. IV cap. 71) s.1

[45] Time Immemorial. Wikipedia

[46] Ibid.

[47] http://www.1066andallthat.com/index.asp

[48] THE SHORT TALK BULLETIN; The Masonic Service Association of the United States; VOL. 31 August 1953 NO. 8

[49] Chapter IV. Acceptable Admittance; Building Free Men; Dr. John S. Nagy (2014)

[50] Peisistratos, the son of Hippocrates, was a tyrant, who ruled in Athens during most of the period between 561 and 527 BCE.

178

[51] Thespis [/ˈθɛspɪs/; Greek: Θέσπις; fl. 6th century – (534 BCE)] of Icaria (present-day Dionysos, Greece), Semi-mythical inventor of Athenian tragedy. Aristotle, later sources say. believed that Thespis added the prologue and speech to choral performance. creating a new genre. This may accurately represent the development of drama from choral lyric (dithyrarnb), but attributing that development to one man probably owes more to the Greek love of finding causes than to fact. Page 600; *The Oxford Companion to Theatre and Performance* edited by Dennis Kennedy; 2010

[52] This, according to the Greek rhetorician Themistius (4th century CE); Thespis - Encyclopedia Britannica

[53] Horace; Wikipedia

[53] Horace, Epistulae, II, 3, 220: "Carmino qui tragico vilem certavit Ars Poetica 275-7

[54] Thespis; Wikipedia

[55] Horace, Epistulae, II, 3, 220

[56] Page 13; Brockett, Oscar Gross; Hildy, Franklin Joseph (2003), History of the theatre (9th, ill ed.), Allyn & Bacon,

[57] Hypokrites (related to our word for hypocrite) also means, less often, "to answer" the tragic chorus. See Weimann (1978, 2); see also Csapo and Slater, who offer translations of classical source material using the term hypocrisis (acting) (1994, 257, 265–267).

[58] Trumbull, Dr. Eric W. "Introduction to Theatre -- The Actor". www.nvcc.edu/home/etrumbull/CST130-ELI/acting.htm

[59] http://freemasonry.bcy.ca/anti-masonry/goat.html

[60] Ezra 6:8-10

[61] Chapter XI – Traveling Men; Building Free Men

[62] The Drama: Its History, Literature and Influence on Civilization, vol. 7. ed. Alfred Bates. London: Historical Publishing Company, 1906. pp. 11-13.

[63] Page 49; The Constitutions of the Free-Masons; James Anderson (1723)

[64] Building Better Builders Workshop Handout

[65] Freemasons for Dummies, by Christopher Hodapp, Wiley Publishing Inc., Indianapolis, 2005, p.85, sec. Hitler and the Nazi

[66] http://phoenixmasonry.org/goose_and_gridiron_ale-house.htm